CORPORATE E-LEARNING

An Inside View of IBM's Solutions

Luther Tai

OXFORD
UNIVERSITY PRESS
2008

OXFORD
UNIVERSITY PRESS

Oxford University Press, Inc., publishes works that further
Oxford University's objective of excellence
in research, scholarship, and education.

Oxford New York
Auckland Cape Town Dar es Salaam Hong Kong Karachi
Kuala Lumpur Madrid Melbourne Mexico City Nairobi
New Delhi Shanghai Taipei Toronto

With offices in
Argentina Austria Brazil Chile Czech Republic France Greece
Guatemala Hungary Italy Japan Poland Portugal Singapore
South Korea Switzerland Thailand Turkey Ukraine Vietnam

Published by Oxford University Press, Inc.
198 Madison Avenue, New York, New York 10016

www.oup.com

Oxford is a registered trademark of Oxford University Press.

Library of Congress Cataloging-in-Publication Data
Tai, Luther, 1948–
Corporate e-learning: an inside view of IBM's solutions / Luther Tai.
    p.   cm.
Includes bibliographical references and index.
ISBN: 978-0-19-531131-0
1. Employees–Training of–Computer-assisted instruction. 2. Organizational learning.
3. Knowledge management. 4. International Business Machines Corporation. I. Title.
HF5549.5.T7T22 2007
658.3'12402854678—dc22   2006038014

9 8 7 6 5 4 3 2 1

Printed in the United States of America
on acid-free paper

Dedicated to my mother, Kuo Hua Li Tai,
and my father, Reverend Doctor Kuang Ming Tai,
for their generosity, love, and devotion

PREFACE

In this book, I examine in depth how e-learning is developed and implemented, and how effectiveness is determined at IBM. In analyzing e-learning at IBM, I refer to other corporations' e-learning practices for comparison purposes. Most of the books that are written about e-learning do not describe in detail how corporate e-learning is done within a specific company. This book fills that gap. Corporate e-learning is so important in today's digital world. The computing power is doubling every 12 to 18 months. Bandwidth is more available and cheaper than ever. People are demanding just-in-time learning and lifetime learning. The notion of access anywhere anytime is just irresistible, but most importantly, e-learning provides strategic and competitive advantages to corporations.

This book discusses the decision criteria used to determine the appropriate level of e-learning. It explores how e-learning is developed and implemented. It examines the extent of e-learning applications at IBM. It explores how the effectiveness of e-learning is measured. IBM's substantial e-learning experience should serve as an important guide for those who are implementing e-learning.

I selected IBM for two primarily reasons. First, it has a great deal of e-learning experience and a large, diversified workforce all over the world. The wide geographical coverage provides an excellent environment to test the extent of applicability of e-learning and its potential difficulties. IBM is an early adopter of e-learning and it already use e-learning widely as a tool for training its workforce. Second, the available access to IBM was a very important consideration. I was able to get permission to interview IBM's e-learning professionals because of my long-standing business relationships with the company. I was able to visit with top-level policy makers, such as the chief learning officer, the chief information officer, human resources professionals, as well as subject- matter experts, designers, Web technologists, instructors, students, and administrators. I believe the trustworthiness of my content has been established because so many people were interviewed.

IBM is a large Fortune 500 company with a strong learning culture. It has over 300,000 employees all over the world. It operates in more than 150 countries. IBM is a renowned global technology company that provides computer hardware, software, and consulting services. It has its own rationale and approach to using e-learning, and it has learned its share of lessons. The experiences of this company provide a unique context for leveraging e-learning to train employees. IBM contributes to the evolution of corporate e-learning in a significant way. IBM represents a rich source of additional knowledge about how corporate e-learning is created.

ACKNOWLEDGMENTS

I want to thank the e-learning professionals and managers from IBM and other corporations for sharing their experiences and insights on corporate e-learning. Their valuable input formed the basis for the publication of this book. I want to thank the faculty at the Graduate School of Education at the University of Pennsylvania for their helpful advice and guidance. I want to thank my family, colleagues, and friends for their encouragement through the process. And I especially want to thank Kevin Burke, Gene McGrath, Bob Yaro, Jerry Hass, Doug Toma, Larry Schall, Matt Hartley, Eli Munzer, Carol Ryan, Doug Lynch, Bob Ubell, George Campbell, Nick Donofrio, Marvin Lazerson, David Juran, Mary-Linda Armacost, John Rauschenberg, Paul Hobson, Dennis Jawor, Joe Lynch, Tony Torphy, Juanita Young, Noah Tai, Lolly Tai, Lois Wooh, Mike Wooh, and Johanna, Nelson, and Lena Tai for their strong support in making it possible to publish this book.

CONTENTS

CORPORATE E-LEARNING

1

INTRODUCTION

Background

The purpose of this research is to understand how IBM develops, implements, and determines the effectiveness of e-learning. Although the e-learning experiences at IBM will be the primary focus of this research, in my analysis of e-learning at IBM, I also refer to other corporations' e-learning practices for comparison purposes.

IBM is a global computer software, hardware, and services company with more than 300,000 employees. Its 2006 revenues were $91.4 billion. Its e-learning course catalog has more than 3,500 courses, and its customers can access more than 14,000 IBM products and solutions. It has received more patents than any other company in the country. It employs 3,000 scientists and engineers in eight labs in six countries and has three Nobel laureates (http://www.ibm.com/ibm/us/). IBM has a large and diverse workforce, including professionals and skilled workers across the country and around the world. They invest substantially in human capital, with a sizable portion of their training budget allocated for e-learning. They spend more than $1 billion annually training its employees (Schettler 2002).

E-learning can be applied to product sales, technical certification, professional competence, business tools, technical skills, new salespeople (sales training), new hires, leadership and legal-compliance training. The experience and lessons learned by IBM and other corporations in these areas serve as a benchmark for corporations initiating e-learning and for those that have already started using e-learning in their training programs.

However, e-learning results from IBM should not be generalized to all corporations and to all e-learning applications. Because of the differences in size, scope, nature of business, and e-learning applications, IBM's experience should be viewed in the context of understanding the objectives of e-learning applications, the budget, the audience, geographical coverage, availability of students time, time to build e-learning solution, shelf life of e-learning solutions, product cycle, and collaboration.

What Is E-Learning?

E-learning, which is short for electronic learning, is defined broadly by Web technology professionals as education and training delivered by an instructor or self-paced from a curriculum database stored on the enterprise local area network (Berry 2000). It refers to anything delivered, enabled, or mediated by electronic technology for the explicit purpose of learning (Hicks 2000). It offers the possibility of learning from information delivered to us electronically (Honey 2001). It is a Web-based, personalized learning experience and provides measurable results (Rich 2001). The broadest definition refers to any distance-learning mode other than a correspondence course with printed material (Mantyla 2001). The clearest definition is found in the book *E-learning: Strategies for Delivering Knowledge in the Digital Age,* where the author says e-learning refers to the use of Internet technologies to deliver a broad array of solutions that enhance knowledge and performance. Solutions are networked, which means instant updating, retrieval, distribution, and delivery to computer users at standard Internet technology (Rosenberg 2001, 28–29). E-learning applications include self-study, instructor-led, Web-based training, knowledge-management, and performance support (Broadbent 2000).

Before the dot-com explosion, many analysts predicted that e-learning would rapidly become widespread and account for the bulk of corporate training. Analysts predicted e-learning would account for 90 percent or more of training in three to four years. That prediction did not materialize. The timetable has since pushed out, but analysts think it will still happen (Piskurich 2003, 19). Domestic online e-learning was expected to grow from $1.1 billion in 1999 to $11.4 billion in 2003 (Gareiss 2001). Most companies are using e-learning on a smaller scale rather than as an enterprise-wide solution. They use e-learning to train sales staff on product rollout and new hires on policies and procedures (Webb 2003b).

E-learning is frequently discussed in the context of asynchronous, synchronous, and blended learning. Asynchronous learning allows learners to have access to the content material anytime and anywhere, at their convenience. E-learning provides a choice of self-paced study, which means that the learner has the choice of when and where to take the lessons (Beamish et al. 2002). The content can be segmented into small modules and the learners can select what modules they wish to learn. Depending on the availability of training time, the length of the module can be adjusted accordingly. Most self-paced e-learning allows learners to preassess their knowledge so they can focus on areas needing improvement. In contrast, the speed of the instructor in a classroom environment might be either too fast or too slow for some learners (Hartley 2001).

Synchronous learning is on-line virtual classroom learning that allows lectures, discussions, and collaboration to be done via Web for users from geographically dispersed areas with no separation of time. The users can participate online with a live instructor and other learners (Maxey 2002, 3). But unlike the self-paced asynchronous learning that can be accessed at any time, the real-time nature of synchronous learning with the real-time participation of the instructor requires that all learners join at a predefined time. It is closer in format to classroom training, which thrives on real-time interaction (Oakes and Rengarajan 2002b).

Blended learning is a combination of the best features of e-learning and classroom learning (Voci and Young 2001). IBM's Basic Blue is an example of a blended learning application in which a leadership development program trains managers worldwide. It combines extensive e-learning modules with on-line support, coaching, and collaboration. A five-day classroom session complements e-learning to round out the learning experience (Henderson 2003, 8).

The choice of method varies depending on the content and speed required for training. If a high level of interactivity is required for training in negotiation skills, e-learning might not deliver the desired level of equivalent interactivity that face-to-face training would provide. Group interactions, culture building, and teamwork are all critical attributes of an overall learning system that is still frequently best suited for classroom experiences (Rosenberg 2001, 120).

Knowledge management is another area that relates to e-learning. It refers to communicating both explicit and tacit information in the appropriate context. A caddy telling a golfer to play a hole fifteen yards long is an example of tacit knowledge. Explicit information is the physical distance to the hole. Knowledge management uses technology but is not by itself technology (http://www.cio.com/summaries/enterprise/knowledge/index.html). By communicating information in the proper context, knowledge makes information useful and meaningful to users (Oakes and Rengarajan 2002a).

Audience

E-learning goes beyond reaching employees. The ultimate goal is not only to train employees for better performance, but to gain greater business advantages as well. Therefore, e-learning is used to train channel customers along the supply chain. Because products and services are becoming more abundant and complicated (an average digital camera has more than 50 functionalities), customers need to be educated. E-learning helps customers become more comfortable with the product and service offerings. Educating customers is a key means to enhance corporate revenues (Aldrich 2000).

How Is Effective E-Learning Defined?

Effective e-learning means different things to different companies and each company has its own way of measuring the effectiveness of e-learning. Effectiveness in performance can mean quality, quantity, or a new way of doing business. It means the benefits of e-learning are outweighing the costs of resources required for implementation. E-learning can result in improved performance, greater speed to market, increased operating efficiency, higher retention and greater return on investment (ROI). Benefits can be savings achieved compared to the cost of existing training programs. Benefits can also come from the ability to perform in a new way that was previously unavailable. For example, by being able to reach the market faster, a salesman has greater opportunity to sell more products, thus achieving more revenue.

Donald Kirkpatrick came up with four levels of evaluation for learning: (1) effectiveness perceived by a trainee; (2) effectiveness as measured by learning evaluation; (3) effectiveness as observed performance improvement; (4) effectiveness as business impact. Kirkpatrick level 1 is a survey of learner satisfaction. Level 2 is an examination of the content to make sure the learner has mastered the content of the training module. Level 3 is an observation of learners translating their knowledge into workplace performance. Level 4 measures ROI (Goldwasser 2001).

Effectiveness can be undermined in a number of ways: at the learner level, if the learner is unprepared and lacks motivation and time; at the product level, if the content is not engaging, relevant, and useful; and at the organizational level, if corporate support structure is absent. E-learning strategy should address issues of technology, learning effectiveness, culture, leadership, justification, organization, talent, and change. (Rosenberg 2001, 32).

Why Is E-Learning Important?

Given fierce global competition, compression of time, expansive territory, demand for just-in-time learning, the streamlined workforce, fiscal concerns, and the rapid movement toward a digital society, e-learning can be an essential component of a corporate training program for many companies attempting to achieve their strategic goals and competitive advantage. The increasing demands for continuous, flexible, lifelong education and the availability of increased bandwidth of more power communication technologies are stimuli for extensive corporate developments in e-learning (Clarke and Hermens 2001). Corporate universities grew from 400 to more than 2,000 in just over a decade (Meister 2001). United States firms with $500 million or more in sales spend, on average, $3.7 million every year on learning and training. (Billington 2003).

E-learning is being used across different sectors of the economy. Some of the biggest movers in the airline and railroad industries are finding that e-learning provides a cost-effective way to keep employees up-to-date on new regulations (Tischell 2002). Ford's North American marketing, sales, and service division is using e-learning to support the nontechnical training needs of 225,000 employees in their dealer channel (Pollitt 2005b). The insurance industry's spending on e-learning will surge (Thomas 2001). Healthcare organizations are going online to learn about health regulations via e-learning (Gillette 2003). The federal government is turning to the Web to train its 1.9 million employees (Thibodeau 2002). A campus-computing project in 2000 revealed that more than 40 percent of all college courses now use Web resources (Kelly 2001). Entrepreneurs and investors have jumped into the world of on-line education, investing some

$6 billion into the sector since 1990 (Grimes 2001). NYU online spent $25 million but attracted only a handful of businesses as clients (Read 2002a). The University of Phoenix's online enrollment, on the other hand, has been on a rapid rise (Wales 2003). Strategic alliances of universities, e-learning providers, and technology companies are offering a vast array of online courses globally. A consortium of universities including Columbia, Stanford, Chicago, and others are offering on-line MBA courses globally through their online Cadean University. Fathom is an e-learning portal established by a group of universities and cultural institutions that offer a diverse portfolio of subjects for lifelong learning. NETg has a portfolio of 600 off-the-shelf training courses in several languages and has a client base that includes many of the global 100 companies (Clarke and Hermens 2001). MIT just launched a bold initiative to speed up the Internet process by making the primary materials for nearly all its 2,000 courses available on the World Wide Web accessible to anyone, anywhere, anytime in the world through its OpenCourseWare portal. This is an effort to share learning with the entire world. MIT also hopes that its classes will be more interactive because the students will come more prepared because they will be able to read the course material beforehand (Vest 2004).

This study will shed light on how e-learning is developed, implemented, and how effectiveness is determined at IBM. The experiences and lessons learned at IBM can be used as a reference for other corporations that are implementing e-learning programs. Managers who are responsible for training their employees can learn how others educate a well-trained workforce and achieve productivity savings. Employees should be interested in e-learning because it provides flexibility, convenience, and a self-directed pace for learning. College and professional educators can learn from corporate practices and apply them effectively in their colleges and in their consulting practices.

What Does E-Learning Add?

This study explores the extent to which e-learning is feasible and the decision criteria that was used to determine the appropriate level of e-learning at IBM. It examines how much e-learning is being developed and implemented and the rationale for the various e-learning applications. It also examines how the effectiveness of e-learning is determined by IBM.

IBM was selected because it has a large number of employees and a global learning community, conditions that lend themselves to e-learning. As such,they have invested substantial resources in implementing e-learning. Because IBM operates in multiple countries and continents, it presents an excellent forum for testing the applicability of e-learning. IBM has its own rationale and approach to using e-learning. IBM went through its own struggles and growing pains. It provides a unique context for leveraging e-learning to train its employees. IBM has been successful in using e-learning in its own right. It contributes to the evolution of corporate e-learning in its own way. IBM is a rich source on how e-learning can be implemented.

Sources of Data Gathering

Personal interviews were the primary source for gathering data. These were conducted with chief learning officers, vice president of on demand learning, chief information officer, chief e-learning architect, learning leaders, designers of content and delivery, administrators, instructors, learners, and business managers. In order to cover these principal players vital to implementing e-learning, I conducted numerous interviews. These interviews were necessary for gathering data for analysis and for answering the research questions on e-learning. In addition, interviewing a wide cross section of e-learning professionals was a way to ensure the trustworthiness of the findings.

Key Questions to Be Explored:
- Why e-learning?
- How is e-learning developed?
- How is e-learning implemented?
- How do corporations determine effectiveness of e-learning?
- What are the lessons learned?

Outline

The first three chapters of this book cover the introduction, literature review, and methodology. Chapter 4 covers e-learning at IBM. It contains description of development, implementation, and effectiveness of corporate e-learning. Chapter 5 is an analysis of e-learning at IBM and how it compares to e-learning practices in other corporations. These are based on analyses of information gathered from interviews, notes, and documents. Chapter 6 points out the lessons learned and best practices in e-learning at IBM and other corporations that can serve as a reference guide for others who are starting e-learning. Many of the findings about fundamental elements of effective e-learning as determined by IBM could be generalized and applied to a variety of corporate and academic areas. Other findings have to be read in the context of the specific circumstances at hand. Chapter 6 is the final, concluding chapter identifying the key findings and observations from this study.

2

LITERATURE REVIEW

Background

The scope of my literature review includes both academic and popular literature on e-learning. Literature review provides a meaningful background on corporate e-learning and is what has led to the need for this study. It uncovers what has already been researched, identifies those experts who are studying the field, and indicates the importance of follow up. Academic or scholarly literature is based on empirical studies. These are based on controlled experiments, surveys, or interviews. Popular literature represents the thoughtful reflection of e-learning experts or advocates. The literature review includes periodicals such as *The Chronicle of Higher Education, Chief Learning Officer*, American Society of Training and Development (ASTD) publications, government publications, industry white papers, books on e-learning, internal documents, and internal studies. Because IBM is the focus of this study, published material on IBM was searched. In addition, unpublished internal documents that were made available were reviewed.

E-learning, similar to any new technology, has gone through significant growing pains in the past decade. In the 1990s, e-learning went through a period of high investment and euphoria, followed by harsh realities of failures and consolidations (Oakes 2002). Many corporations, in their rush to implement e-learning, took missteps because of lack of familiarity with e-learning and miscalculations of the amount of resources required for implementation. Because e-learning is a new and unexplored area for many corporations, it is not surprising that mistakes occurred (Weaver 2002).

The American Society of Training and Development publishes a compilation of corporate learning data each year, and in their most recent report, growth in e-learning is shown to have slowed down. E-learning as a percent of corporate training dropped from 9.1 percent in 1997 to 8.4 percent by 1999 (Coleman 2001). The growth rate moved up slightly to 8.8 percent in 2000 (Elswick 2002). Some experts are still expecting growth rates to accelerate. Jefferies & Company Incorporated forecast e-learning to be as much as 22 percent of the corporate training market by 2005 (Sauer 2001).

Contrary to the perception that e-learning is a cheap method of training, experience shows that it is very costly to implement e-learning (Rubenstein 2003). E-learning suppliers struggled in 2002. Corporate cutbacks, vendor performance, and difficult economic times hampered the high growth projections for the industry (Oakes 2003a). However, history has shown us that technology is ubiquitous. Therefore, in spite of difficulties encountered, experts feel that it's just a matter of time until everyone will find himself or herself using e-learning whether as a student, instructor, developer, or administrator (Broadbent 2000).

E-learning, classroom training, on the job training, mentoring, and experiential learning are the various ways employees acquire knowledge and enhance job skills. Because of the complexity of development of human skills, there is no single approach that can provide a complete solution for employee skill development. E-learning is by no means the silver bullet. The key is to blend the best features of e-learning and classroom training. The challenge for corporations is to use multiple options best suited for learners based on their particular needs, preferences, and learning environment (Weaver 2002). E-learning begins with careful consideration of the rationale for using it and the hurdles faced in development and implementation of e-learning. The rationale should include clear objectives and the costs/benefits of e-learning. The development phase should consider content, design, technology, infrastructure, and target audience. Implementation should include careful preparation of learners and instructors for e-learning, and it should provide the learners with sufficient corporate support. Effectiveness of e-learning should include examination of performance indicators, and such feedback should be used to improve the overall process. Each step in developing e-learning is an integral part of the whole process, and these steps should be considered jointly. E-learning should reflect a thorough understanding of the whole enterprise (Sparta 2002). Failure can occur at any of the steps along the way.

Corporations, in their rush to implement e-learning, often place too much emphasis on the *e* and too little on the *learning* part of e-learning (Imel 2002). Technology is not meant to be used for the sake of technology alone. There has to be matching desire on the part of learners to accept e-learning. Ultimately, it is what learners learn—not the technology they use to learn it—that matters (Coleman 2001).

E-learning should not be blindly accepted unless quality, technology, access, and other relevant issues are sufficiently addressed (Imel 2002). Some corporations have aggressively moved toward an environment in which the majority of learning happens via e-learning (Oakes 2003b). Others are less willing to make such a move. E-learning is not yet a solution for everyone. Some people prefer to learn in a classroom environment (Coleman 2001). Some companies are still reluctant to channel their resources to this area, perhaps because they do not know how to adapt this new approach to learning (Yeoh 2001).

This literature review explores the reasons corporations choose e-learning as an option for learning and how e-learning is developed and implemented and how effectiveness is evaluated. IBM is an early adopter of e-learning. Their experiences can benefit those corporations that are just getting started (Hassett 2002).

Why Do Corporations Use E-Learning?

Corporations using e-learning do so for a variety of reasons. They do it for strategic reasons, accessibility, speed, geography, attraction and retention, productivity and investment purposes.

Strategic Reasons

Educating employees proves to be a guaranteed ticket to success (Rianhard 2002). Corporations recognize that human capital is their most valuable resource and that training will increase their organization's effectiveness (King 2001). As corporations are pressured for greater profits and tighter budgets, management is paying increasingly more attention to employee education. According to a Merrill Lynch study, corporations with a workforce with a 10 percent higher educational attainment level realized an 86 percent higher productivity (Yeoh 2001). Corporations that use e-learning to make the connection between learning and strategy facilitate the achievement of their business goals (Henry 2002). Jack Welch, former CEO of GE, once said that "An organization's ability to learn and translate that learning into action is the ultimate competitive advantage." GE's corporate university at Crotonville serves as a model of how companies can successfully use learning to impact their business strategy (Henry 2002). GE invests $1 billion in training each year. Learning is a vital part of GE culture and GE managers are graded on how they perform in training their employees (General Electric Company 2002).

Ted Hoff, IBM's chief learning officer said, "Today more than ever learning is a vital component of business growth. Learning initiative helps the company develop the best talent in the industry and it directly enables business to win and grow in a competitive market place" (Hoff 2003).

Aware of the importance of learning, some companies spend vast amounts of money on e-learning without understanding what types of results to expect. They do training simply because it is good to do (Waller 2001). But training is not an end in itself and must be purposeful to help corporations achieving their business goals. The business case should include improved performance, greater efficiency, higher sales of products and services, lower costs, growing profits and a higher return on investment (Egan 2002).

Cisco Systems acquires a new partner every two and a half weeks. Prior to e-learning, account managers had to consult hundreds of internal websites to keep up with acquisition information. Now they have a single e-learning portal as a primary source for learning (Galagan 2001).

According to Marc Rosenberg, a leading figure in the world of e-learning and an author of a best-selling book, any good business case must justify the investment in e-learning in three ways. First, it must meet business needs, such as responsiveness to rapid change and support for field force. Second, it must be more economical than other forms of learning. Third, it must treat knowledge not just as a cost, but also as an asset (Rosenberg 2001).

Accessibility

One of E-learning's greatest selling points is flexible, round-the-clock online access to any number of courses (Gareiss 2001). IBM recognizes that their employees value flexibility and want lifelong learning beyond classroom learning (IBM Annual Report 2002).

However, flexibility has a major drawback. It is self-directed study and requires high levels of motivation. Self-study is unfamiliar to adults who are more accustomed to instructor-led classroom training. Classroom training creates an environment in which people stop work and focus on training. It doesn't prepare learners to learn in isolation. Without motivation, learners may not complete e-training. George Piskurich, a leading figure in the world of e-learning design, remarked, "We got into this idea that if we build it, they will come. We heard too many Field of Dreams processes going on. And they may actually come, but they don't stay very long." Piskurich suggested allowing workers to complete their e-learning on the job without interrupting them. He said that requiring employees to train on their own time signals that it's not part of their job and, therefore, that it's not important (Elswick 2002). Employees are also spending more time working and will resist e-learning if they have to keep the same workloads. It is problematic if management is not willing to implement e-learning because they fear it will reduce productivity (Weaver 2002). If employees want to train at their desks and a manager asks them to work on something else, e-learning will fail (Hassett 2002). There is a need for a shift in corporate attitude to accept employees learning at their desks (Coleman 2001).

Besides employees, another significant audience that benefits from the accessibility of e-learning is customers. E-learning can be a way to help customers become more comfortable with the product and service offerings. Products and services are becoming more abundant and complicated. An average digital camera now has more than 50 functionalities. Further, in order to answer customers' questions, corporations also need to make sure that their channel partners are well informed. Using e-learning to train channel partners is a way to avoid the hassle of expensive travel or the monotony of classroom courses. Information can be updated frequently, and channel partners can be certified in certain areas through online tests that grade them on skills learned (Cummings 2001). IBM's Learning Services provides external customers with course offerings amounting to two million education days per year (Torode 1999). IBM educates channel partners with online sessions that last anywhere from 30 minutes to the whole day. IBM provides training sessions on new products such as ThinkPad or X Series E-servers (Cummings 2001). Educating customers is a key means to enhance corporate revenues (Aldrich 2000). Ohanian of Vuepoint noted the criticality of time to market. Rapid transfer of knowledge to sales channel is vital, particularly in this era of frequent market changes and complex product mix (Harris 2003).

Size, Geography, and Speed

As more regions of the world are interconnected by wire, and computing and Internet access costs are rapidly decreasing, e-learning is becoming a more feasible method of learning (Piskurich 2003, 75). Corporations are finding a need to move to e-learning because of the speed of change in today's information-driven economy (Verespej 2001). There are more and more desktop and laptop computers, and there is more bandwidth. In 1965, Gordon More made the prediction that the number of transistors that would fit on a chip would double every 12 to 18 months. This means that in 10 years, the low-end PC will cost about $150 and offer 8 GB of RAM and 1.8 Terabytes of storage space (Kruse 2003).

E-learning is used to minimize travel and to distribute information to a large number of people quickly (Groves 2002). Traditional training simply can take too long to reach large groups. GE has to reach over 300,000 employees in 28 business units in regional offices all over the world. GE standardized its new hire orientation program for thousands of employees via e-learning to provide them with access (Schank 2002, 141). IBM has to reach more than 300,000 employees among 8 separate business units in various regions around the world. IBM employees are trained worldwide within a short time frame via e-learning (Mantyla 2001, 31).

Cisco Systems uses e-learning to train 10, 000 engineers and account managers in their field, 40,000 channel partners who sell their products in 132 countries, and hundreds of thousands of ultimate customers who use Cisco products. Rapid learning for these audiences is key to Cisco's growth strategy (Galagan 2001). Crown, maker of beverage cans, used e-learning to train thousands of employees on regulation compliance (Hollis 2003). Ernst & Young used e-learning to reach 80,000 workers worldwide. The Credit Union National Association used e-learning to train 10,000 credit unions on the security provisions in the PATRIOT Act (Driscoll 2003). Delta rolled out its "Our Airline, Our Business" program in May 2002, with 48 facilitators delivering more than 1,100 sessions to 33,000 employees in 32 cities between May and December 2002 (Salopek 2003).

Bristol-Myers Squibb used e-learning to train more than 3,500 sales representatives and managers and gained sales days by keeping its representatives and managers in the field (Del Vecchio and Bonthrone 2003). Braxton (formerly Deloitte Consulting) trained its 15,000 employees with speed and efficiency without removing their employees from assignments (Gold 2003). A. T. Kearney used e-learning to reach their consultants scattered across 60 offices and 30 countries. Morrison of A. T. Kearney said that e-learning allows self-selection and thus eliminates unnecessary training (Harris 2003).

The key principles behind e-learning are scalability, accessibility, and timeliness (Clarke and Hermens 2001). Scalability means that the software has the ability to provide access to a growing number of users (Devi 2001).

Attraction/Retention

Corporations are relying on e-learning as a way to invest in their employees to ensure greater job satisfaction, enhance career development, and foster loyalty (Evans 2002). Electronics companies in particular use e-learning to attract and retain a highly qualified workforce (Rich 2001). At TechOnLine, an e-learning company, engineers have the opportunity to enhance their technical skills and create e-learning programs (van der Pool 2001). Procter and Gamble's offering of e-learning to a large number of low-skilled workers all over the world signals that it cares about its staff and retention. Swedish Bank SEB used e-learning in mergers to help newly acquired businesses quickly get up to speed with its culture (Coleman 2001).

Productivity

E-learning often lowers training costs by avoiding travel and the associated costs (Hequet and Johnson 2003). However, lower cost should not be achieved at the expense of quality. Rich Wellins, senior vice president at Development Dimensions International, said, "I still see the primary driver being cost, not quality. It boils down to a pure cost decision made by the CEO and CFO"(Oakes 2003c).

Savings result from the elimination of instructor's fees, facilities charges, or travel costs associated with the classroom learning. IBM used e-learning to train 6,318 managers worldwide at one third of the classroom cost (Mantyla 2001, 31). IBM offers five times the content it did prior to e-learning at one third of the cost and saves $200 million annually, according to Brandon Hall from a research of e-learning practices at IBM (Verespej 2001). IBM and Microsoft have tens of millions dollars of savings in hotel and travel bills (Webdale 2003). Scottish Power achieved 70 percent return on investment in their health and safety instruction course (Pollitt 2005c). Kodak used e-learning to reduce instructor costs, facilities costs, travel expenses, and cost associated with the classroom learning

(Stim 2002). Braxton used e-learning to reduce training cost from $7,500 per employee to $3,000 (Gold 2003). Reynolds and Reynolds saved $1 million during the first year of e-learning. Cisco Systems Inc. realized a 24 percent increase in efficiency (Gale 2002). Verizon realized its value in terms of cost reduction and performed an exhaustive ROI study, finding that its return on investment was conservatively over 822 percent (Munzer 2002).

Savings such as reduction in training budgets and materials, travel, instructors, physical facilities, administrative time, and hours of lost productivity when employees are off-site can be determined without difficulty. However, soft areas such as employee satisfaction, retention, and morale are not always so easily measured (Harris 2003).

Although substantial savings can result by avoiding travel and associated expenses, an even greater amount of gains can be achieved because the employees have more time to spend in the workplace and can produce more products and services. E-learning, which is just-in-time learning, can help a company quickly train the remaining employees to pick up the work vacated by laid off workers. When production is slow, workers can do telemarketer work and then return to production when demand picks up (Egan 2002).

At Cisco Systems' manufacturing branch, assembly workers have not seen a classroom since 1999 and have access to e-learning right on the factory floor. The company is achieving savings of $1 million per quarter in improved process and an 80 percent increase in speed to competence. Cisco performed a controlled experiment on 200 employees for certification training with one-half attending live classes and one-half using e-learning. The e-learners had a 10 percent better passing rate in this single experiment (Galagan 2001).

E-Learning can decrease costs, improve business responsiveness, customize training, and provide valuable customer service (Rosenberg 2001, 30). Many corporations are only beginning to realize the potential cost savings in moving from traditional training to e-learning. Some companies have started measurement programs to prove e-learning's positive impact on customer service, productivity, and sales (Berry 2000).

A four-year study by the American Society for Training and Development showed that firms that invest $1,500 per employee in training compared to those that spend $125 experience, on average, 24 percent higher gross profit margins and 218 percent higher income per employee (Rosenberg 2001, 216).

The goal of e-learning measurements is to create a link between e-learning and how a company now does X, Y, and Z better (Krell 2002).

Investment

Many people expect e-learning to be less expensive than traditional delivery methods. In reality, however, it has proven to be quite expensive. Developing customized online courseware is costly. Typically, e-learning service providers charge from $10,000 to $60,000 to develop one hour of online instruction (Hassett 2002). According to Elliott Masie, a recognized proponent of e-learning, creating content and courseware incurs substantial costs for planning, infrastructure, systems integration, ongoing communications, and marketing required to ensure use by targeted learners. Corporations often overlook those costs and make purchasing decisions based solely on the cost of course content. This is not to say that e-learning cannot be cost effective, especially with many users in multiple locations. However, it would not be realistic to expect a meticulously planned and implemented system to come cheaply (Weaver 2002). The Home Depot invested hundreds of development hours to train 90,000 associates on forklift operations. It creates a positive initial experience so learners will return for additional training in the future (Vam Dam 2004). URS Corp. invested 4,000 person hours and another 16,000 consultation hours to devise a project-management course to train its 15,000 employees worldwide (Thomas 2001). Because of potentially high investments, a short pilot can be tested and, after demonstrated ROI, the project can then be expanded (Webb 2003a).

How Is E-Learning Developed?

To develop e-learning, target audience, content, design, technology and infrastructure are factors that need to be considered. The content has to be relevant and learners should be able to apply what's learned at the workplace. Technology and infrastructure have to be suitable for delivery of content to learners.

E-Learning versus Classroom Learning

Despite a growing use of e-learning, classroom training still is the predominant means for corporate training. Based on a recent Development

Dimensions International (DDI) survey, more than two thirds of leadership training is still done in classrooms. This result suggests that e-learning will take a long time to or may never replace classroom training entirely. People are social learners and are accustomed to learning in groups. They prefer to exchange ideas and interact with peers face-to-face. Classroom training provides that experience whereas e-learning generally cannot (Weaver 2002). E-learning, however, provides online communicating in groups via bulletin board, discussion board, chat rooms, and other electronic mechanism. It provides collaboration and social interaction when each participant takes on a role, such as leader or moderator, and all work toward a common purpose. It provides humor through graphics and colors to motivate employees to learn and to break down cultural barriers (Burns 2005). Online or virtual classroom learning also allows private conversations among participants and between participants and instructors through instant messaging or private chat without disturbing the flow of the class. However, there is still the problem of misinterpreting words and messages (Piskurich 2003, 177). In a virtual classroom, the instructor cannot see the body language of learners to know if the instruction is hitting the mark. Learner feedback has to be obtained by other methods, such as by polling the participants (Oakes and Rengarajan 2002c).

E-learning provides learners with a means to repeat parts of a program that aren't clear to them. Great-West, an insurance company, realized the value of repetition by enabling its new sales reps to go back to product information as many times as they needed to improve their product knowledge. This is more helpful than the classroom training, which allows learners to be exposed to product training only one time. E-learning also provides consistency in training. New sales reps can access the same courses regardless of when or where their training occurred (Franklin 2003).

E-learning can increase the time to capability by reducing the time it takes to train employees on new products and services. According for *Fortune Magazine*, training that customarily takes six to nine months can be compressed to two to three weeks, thereby assuring quicker time to market for products (Pantazis 2002). In an interview, John Chambers of Cisco Systems said, "E-learning helps eliminate barriers of time, distance and socioeconomic status, so individuals are empowered to take charge of their own lifelong learning (Galagan 2001)." Some learners can learn more effectively on their own and achieve comparable results in a shorter time than they would in an instructor led class (Zenger and Uehlein 2001).

E-learning allows learners to progress at their own pace and to complete learning at times best suited for their schedule. Learners can approach learning from a common starting point. They don't have to hold back others or become bored by a slower pace. Peter Drucker, one of the most sought after teachers of our time and an advocate of e-learning, recognized that he could reach only so many people through the classroom. He embraced e-learning with the assumption that the trainer is obsolete. Drucker said, "The trainer is built into the teaching (or learning) device." Roger Schank, director of the Institute for Learning Sciences at Northwestern University and another e-learning advocate said, "Classrooms couldn't possibly exist today. Centuries ago, they made sense: one literate person reading to the illiterate from what might have been the town's only book." But technology and times have changed. The ideal of one-on-one instruction is not practical in today's classrooms. "A computer can give you more one-on-one interaction than a human can when that human has 30 other humans to deal with," he says. "In a classroom, people who are curious, inquisitive, and questioning take up too much time" (Galagan 2000).

Not all corporations have turned to e-learning yet. Some still cling to traditional classroom learning as primary mode of training. Zenger and Uehlein postulated that the pattern of instructor-led learning is established in almost everyone's school experience and connects with the past. Thus, learners prefer to learn in social settings, and classrooms provide opportunities for learners to interact and get feedback. (Zenger and Uehlein 2001).

Content/Design

Designing e-learning includes considerations for content, context, consistency, repeatability, instructions, elicitation, support, customer service, evaluation, and collaboration (Evans 2002). Global considerations should include language, time zones and cultural differences.

The quality of the content is a significant factor contributing to the effectiveness of e-learning (Weaver 2002). In a classroom environment, a gifted teacher can still have an impact even if the content he is teaching is weak. However, in the e-learning world, weak content cannot be compensated for (Taylor 2002). Content can be enhanced by incorporating the qualities of live role play with computer simulations. Aldrich of Simulearn said that authentic and relevant scenarios that tap users' emotions and force them to act should be considered (Powell 2002). In 1997, IBM's CEO, Lou Gerstner, commissioned e-learning to be designed with practical scenarios for users to develop coaching skills. Gerstner felt that the ability to coach employees was essential for good management (Schank 2002, 32).

Simulation was once used primarily by airlines, armies, and governments, but in recent years, it has been a higher profile tool among corporations. The strongest selling point in simulation lies in its fundamental principle of learning through experience. Most simulation e-learning today comes with a learning management system that gives users immediate feedback and tracks their performance (Johne 2003). Simulators have several elements that set them apart from other e-learning experiences. They include built-in realism, highly interactive experience, opportunity for learners to make safe mistakes and get immediate feedback, and repeated practice to achieve competence (Zenger and Uehlein 2001). Simulation provides corporations with the opportunity to review a learner's capability. King said that it is important to review what learners do, what they can do, and what you want them to do. The closer the match, the more learners will be satisfied and the better their performance will be (King 2001). One frequently discussed approach is to build organizational learning into the business. That is, to create an environment in a culture that encourages knowledge sharing, supports a climate of learning from mistakes, and assures that what is learned is incorporated into future initiatives (Rosenberg 2001, 14).

Wang used a pedagogical model to successfully pilot an e-learning program. The model allowed the workers to learn through three levels of knowledge: know what (introductory knowledge), know how (action-oriented skills through simulations) and know why (accumulation of personal experience, interaction with peers) (Wang 2002).

Traditionally, the level of training is judged by the number of hours of classroom training, but e-learning training is judged on the basis of relevance, rather than class hours. Motorola, for example, stopped requiring its 110,000 employees to complete 40 hours of training each year. "To finish a course isn't the issue," says Jill Brosig. "What you want someone to do is go in there and get the information they need. The advantage e-learning provides you is you can go in and just get those pieces that fill in the gaps of what you need to know" (Elswick 2002). Users want something short and digestible. Citigroup's Burt says, "Stop building multi-hour, multi-subject courses. Get size down, and get courses out quickly. Don't just convert class materials to the Web; design the material for Web delivery.

Courses must be engaging, thought-provoking and should also include some eye candy" (Hassett 2002).

Based on interviews with vendors, businesses are now focusing on cost effectiveness and solutions to real training issues (Bolch 2002). Benedet of SkillSoft viewed content as addressing specific business solutions such as call-center training, sales training, IT certification and leadership (Harris 2003).

Although it may be easy to purchase technology, it is far more difficult to innovate the content and effectively deliver it to the learners through this technology (Smedberg 2004). E-learning is more than designing courses laden with content and putting them on the Web. In reality, it is more about connecting the minds of the people in an organization in order to move faster and ultimately be more productive (Oakes 2002).

Learner Consideration

E-learning is not just about technology and delivery of content. It requires understanding what is going on with the learners and how to support them. Significant investment in pedagogical design will enhance realization of greater possibilities of e-learning (Macpherson, Homan, and Wilkinson 2005). In addition, learner support includes online help and diagnostics systems to track how learners and instructors are doing relative to intended goals (Mauger 2002).

One potential issue that corporations may encounter is a lack of motivation on the part of the learner. This is especially true for those who were sent by their companies in the past to a resort for a week of training (Hobson 2001). The problem with asking learners whether they would like to learn online or through more conventional means is that there will be a variety of responses. Some people will reject e-learning simply because it is new. Others, more open-minded, will not understand online learning deeply enough to weigh its attributes against potential disadvantages.

Calling on the work of a University of New Mexico professor, Everett M. Rogers, IBM paid particular attention to five distinct predictors of innovation acceptance: relative advantage, compatibility, complexity, trialability, and observability. Relative advantage includes such things as profitability, speed, social, prestige, and effectiveness. Compatibility is the degree that it's viewed as consistent with existing values and past experiences of potential adopters. Simplicity is perceived as relative ease of use. Trialability means the opportunity to try an innovation with no requirement for continued use. This gives users a chance to see how it works under their own situations and conditions. Observability is the degree to which the results of an innovation are visible to others. Nancy Lewis demonstrated how IBM's Big Blue program for leadership development satisfies these five attributes and why it is, therefore, successful (Lewis and Orton 2000).

E-learning should use situations and challenges similar to those e-learners will face. IBM's Basic Blue features other managers as they struggle with challenges that are inherent to their positions (Little 2003a). Basic Blue is an e-learning program designed for training 30,000 new and experienced managers in more than 50 countries each year. This replaced the traditional classroom training for managers. This program has a series of interventions that stretch over a period of 10 months. It's available 24/7 and allows a new first-line manager to achieve mastery of skills required to be an effective leader at IBM. It also has a five-day learning lab devoted to establishing a peer network, developing face-to-face teamwork and collaborating and building on the management skills that began with online learning. The first 30 days of QuickView teaches the appropriate actions managers should take with their employees and line managers in different situations. The new manager is supported by online material in a LearningSpace media center along with an online coaching simulator. The new manager works through a series of self-directed modules and online simulations (Henderson 2003, 8–10). There are eight 20-minute scenarios that draw learners into discussions on practical problems. The characters appear and describe to simulation users problems encountered by real employees at IBM. Each response has pros and cons, and the user can talk to the expert for opinions. At this point, it transforms into a one-on-one discussion. Thus, the Basic Blue program directly addresses the decisions and questions of learners.

A corporation must also determine whether e-learning will be compatible with its corporate culture (Piskurich 2003, 74). Workplace barriers are often based in cultural resistance (Beamish et al. 2002). Not every learning intervention will work in every corporation. An adventure team building course on the Coast of Maine might not work in a no-nonsense business culture (Ready 2002). Understanding the cultural complexity of a corporation will assist a company in maximizing the full potential activity in e-learning (Piers 2003).

Delivery

Technology makes e-learning possible, but it's people and their perform-ance that matter. Technology together with considerations for social needs and workplace context will affect learner's motivation and ability to learn (Servage 2005).

Despite how e-learning has penetrated into the workplace, technology can still make people uncomfortable. Change that comes from adoption of new technology makes people uneasy. E-learning requires changes in culture and workplace behavior, and it needs corporations to become more competitive. People who champion the use of e-learning need to be involved from the beginning. Throughout implementation, their opinions and concerns should be respected (Weaver 2002). People with technical expertise should be involved in the selection and implementation of e-learning. Decision makers often make hasty purchasing decisions without assessing available technology and securing the buy-in of technical experts. Technology is an enabler, and it should be limited to precisely what is required and not one bit more. Materials delivered over the Web must work properly on hundreds or thousands of PCs, each potentially configured differently by owners (Hassett 2002). Employees need to have access to PCs for e-learning. Appropriate infrastructure, bandwidth, standards, support, and technology are also required. Speed of delivery is becoming as important as what is delivered (Piskurich 2003, 191). The focus is not on how elaborate the technology, but what technology is needed to be optimally effective (Read 2002b).

In the face of bandwidth restrictions, best practices are less likely to come in the form of one big answer, but rather in many smaller ones. The challenges are more about learning to combine the design side with the technology side that will give the greatest return for the least time and investment. There is a need to find feasible ways to keep bandwidth restrictions from hindering an operation while still producing engaging and effective content (Maisto and Rajendran 2002). Efficient delivery of e-learning requires the cooperation and interaction of training and IT managers—something that might not have been required before (Beamish, et al. 2002). Design should consider who the end users are, the location where they're working and their connection speed (Maisto and Rajendran 2002). When learning is Web based, selection and implementa-tion must include members of the information technology group. IT professionals can provide the necessary technical specifications and help establish a realistic implementation time line (Weaver 2002).

Leading-edge technology is important but not critical. Appropriate instructional design is more significant (Henderson 2003, 83). The power of corporate learning technology is its ability to leverage corporate knowledge to increase worker productivity and ultimately business performance (Oakes 2003b).

Blended Learning

Because learners can repeat the subject until it's fully mastered, e-learning content can be consistent in a way that human instructions may not be. Classroom training, on the other hand, offers a familiar and comfortable method that learners are used to. It is an environment in which learners can get immediate feedback through teachers, group discussions, and team presentations. Blended learning captures the strengths of both e-learning and classroom learning (Voci and Young 2001). It mixes different learning methods to optimize the effects of each (Bagshaw and Bagshaw 2002).

Blended learning enables learners to arrive on the first day of class already prepared to discuss the concepts and how they apply to work situations. It expects learner preparedness and it allows social interactions. Blended learning considers the target audience, skills, content, technical resources, personnel resources, and budget and time constraints (Piskurich 2003).

IBM developed a four-tier model called "The E-Learning Model." This model blends e-learning with classroom learning. The first three tiers are done online, whereas the fourth tier is a classroom interactive session. The first tier covers information and awareness. The second tier covers understanding of work practices. The third tier involves collaborative learning through simulations. The final, fourth tier is the face-to-face intervention (Sloman 2002, 46). Similarly, Great-West realized that it would be far less expensive if sales reps could learn about products on their own, while out in the field. The costly face-to-face training time can only be reserved for strategic soft-skills training that reps need to sell the products (Franklin 2003). When face-to-face interaction is required, instructor-led sessions are still preferable (Waller 2001). Face-to-face learning can promote social interaction and discussion of ideas in a complex way that computers cannot. Brennan of IDC said that when developing a salesperson's ability to negotiate and handle face-to-face encounters, teaching by experienced pros couldn't be replaced by Internet. Role playing for different selling situations requires learners to get direct feedback from a seasoned instructor (Thomas 2001). Learners build a trusting relationship when dealing one-on-one. Nonverbal cues give an early indication of needed additional support. Emotional intelligence plays a part. Learners can also gain another's perspective. E-learning, however, in no way hinders the opportunity for traditional training. It is not about eliminating expensive classroom training, but rather about determining its appropriateness. The two methods can be optimally combined (King 2001). Developing blended solutions can be a challenge. Corporations tend to have internal expertise in either instructor-led training or e-learning. Most traditional organizations have great capability in instructor-led training. Conversely, some high-tech companies are inclined toward Web delivery. There are not many cases in which both capabilities exist in equal portions. This means that a company's employees will be predisposed to one approach or the other, which challenges the development of truly blended solutions (Zenger and Uehlein 2001).

Sourcing

Corporations can develop e-learning internally, outsource it, or do it in partnership with another entity. For internal development, corporations need to assess if they have all the skill sets, technology, instructional system designs, graphics, and content specialists required. They also need to consider downtime, noncore job skills, and the difficulties of retaining sought after skills. Trainers can promote implementation of e-learning by partnering with IT, because IT personnel tend to be the most enthusiastic of e-learners (Barron 2000).

Internal e-learning can be created centrally at the corporate level or it can be developed at the business unit level. Some issues are common across the corporation, whereas others are directly related to individual business units. Training that is suited for individual business units can be initiated and sponsored by the business unit itself. Deference is often given to business units because they are more familiar with their business. The corporate arm provides consultation and support, and makes sure that instructional design is appropriate and standardization of hardware and software is maintained. At Verizon, the e-learning development group within the training department is responsible for developing e-learning courses. This development team works with in-house experts to develop e-learning courses (George and McGee 2003).

Outsourcing is also a viable option, especially if IT is either not equipped or overwhelmed. Because of the complexity of integrating disparate learning technologies, and the amount of administration and maintenance for those systems, outsourcing e-learning may be an attractive option. Outsourcing has its difficulties as well. It is difficult to outsource training when the training function is dispersed in corporations (Oakes 2003c). It's not down the hall and there is less control of it. Trying to force a solution into an environment without knowing the corporation's business needs could lead to disaster. There are vendors who offer standard solutions, rather than customized ones. Their business initiatives are often not tied to the business problem that needs to be solved (Hartley 2000).

Partnerships are a third option for corporations looking to develop e-learning programs. Colleges are engaging in a wide variety of partnerships with corporations, which may include conducting on-site courses, sharing research, and creating custom made degree programs (Meister 2001). Some colleges and large corporations are collaborating to create online graduate degree programs that meet companies' specific needs. Babson College started a masters degree program in business administration for Intel workers. The University of Texas at Austin plans to release an online masters of science degree in science technology in commercialization for students who will work at IBM. The students solve programs and complete projects that relate directly to their companies, which helps the students learn material that can be immediately beneficial (Carnevale 2002).

Sjogren and Fay offered some suggestions on how to create partnership options for online offerings. These include being clear about the purpose for offering Internet-based courses; separating goals into short, medium, and longer term, with consideration for starting small; benchmarking and learning from others' mistake; tracking costs and providing support services for both students and instructors. Technical assistance, library resources, and student services, such as tutoring, all can be obtained through partnerships (Sjogren and Fay 2002).

How Is E-Learning Implemented?

Precious corporate resources are wasted when learners don't use e-learning and when corporate objectives are not met. Involving users in planning and implementation is a prerequisite to e-learning success (Weaver 2002).

Marketing E-Learning

Corporations may not realize the importance of internal publicity and promotion to the implementation of e-learning. Getting buy-in from learners is important so that they'll be motivated to apply the learning. Without this buy-in, no amount of training will have much of a chance to improve performance (Weaver 2002). Even if e-learning is made available, it doesn't mean learners will come. Rebecca Ray of Skandia discussed the importance of making employees excited about e-learning through internal marketing (McConnell 2002).

Moving from an environment that is 100 percent classroom based to one based on e-learning can be a significant cultural change. It is difficult to change the mindset that the learner is not being trained unless there's a trainer standing in a classroom delivering the material (Hollis 2003). At Citigroup's e-product development group, every e-learning rollout includes internal marketing with advice for other departments on how to market their courses (Hassett 2002).

At Xerox, posters in local languages, menu cards, brochures, advertisements, inserts in bill slips are some of the eye catching and simple ways of marketing e-learning across their organization (Ettinger 2005).

Even employees at a technology company like IBM had some initial reservation. IBM Management Development was faced with a problem of rolling out a new learning intervention called Basic Blue for managers. A random sample of 63 new IBM managers was surveyed, and the survey indicated that they preferred classroom learning over online learning. However, when Professor Moon of Harvard was commissioned by IBM to conduct postprogram interviews, she found that the respondents preferred using e-learning to access information material from their home or office rather than being in a classroom setting. On the other hand, they preferred learning the behavior skills in a classroom environment. Respondents indicated that they preferred an approach that was best suited to content (Sloman 2002).

Magner of Wachovia Securities said that good internal marketing starts in the development phase by involving your target audience in the creation of the e-learning program. She said that showing the success of a small pilot is another internal marketing tactic that can be used (McConnell 2002).

Cable and Wireless, an international telecommunications company, uses marketing campaigns including mailings, road shows, and intranet news to educate employees on available e-learning courses (Pollitt 2005a).

Peer-group influence can be a more important marketing tool than a mandate in e-learning. Early adopters can be champions of e-learning (Piskurich 2003, 342). Kodak used a grassroots change agent approach for e-learning adoption. Instead of a big rollout, grassroots change agents were used to start the program in the Latin American region. More than 100 individuals were trained on the applications and the benefits of e-learning and even simple problem-solving techniques. These change agents were not professional trainers but were more like "super users." As a result, more than 80 percent of the Latin American region is registered on e-campus (Stim 2002).

Still, some experts say the best way is to require and monitor course completion if corporations want to make sure that a course is fully used by everyone (Hassett 2002). To prepare learners, trainers provide them with orientation, instruction books, schedules, a help desk number and awards (Piskurich 2003, 342).

Corporations can encourage acceptance by creating a teaching culture where everyone has an obligation to teach others. As a classroom instructor, a seminar presenter, or a mentor, participating in the creation and delivery of instruction is not only rewarding, but it also can change an entire firm's perspective on learning (Rosenberg 2001, p. 188).

Supporting Learners

Lack of familiarity, self-motivation, time, and support are significant obstacles for learners. In order to keep learners from quitting an online session, e-learning programs should guide them toward appropriate choices and avoid placing them in situations in which they will lose confidence. It's important to provide prerequisite information and to help online learners assess whether they are qualified for the experience (Little 2003b).

Corporations need to assess basic literacy, computer literacy, motivation levels of learners and their potential problems. The concern for ROI should not be so overriding that its heavy emphasis is at the expense of learner's experiences (Holman and Macpherson 2005). Understanding employees' attitudes and behaviors toward e-learning is important for the rate of adoption of this technology (Gallaher and Wentling 2004).

Distractions such as beepers, fatigue, eye strain, time lag in response, and equipment problems also need to be taken into consideration (Piskurich 2003, 101).Dedicated time and freedom from disturbance are required for e-learning. Using headphones while e-learning is in progress will deter interruptions (Beamish et al. 2002). Employees should not view e-learning as something to be developed on their own time (Hollis 2002). At Cisco Systems, employees can put up yellow police tapes to signal that they are busy learning and they recognize that learning is a valued part of the job (Galagan 2001). Presseau of United Airlines said it's important to have the support of the managers and supervisors of employees because they are the ones who carve out employees' time for training. Training should be tailored to the needs of individual organizations. Training at a hub airport is different from training for a smaller airport. United Airlines gives people decision trees rather than tests to assess their abilities to avoid a huge turnoff. It's important that trainees have a good experience because word of mouth has a significant impact in attracting or detracting people from e-learning (McConnell 2002). For an old-line industry with a lot of older employees, extra time may have to be spent to make them comfortable with online training (Egan 2002). For instance, for automobile workers, making an assumption that everyone knows how to operate a computer and will be receptive to training on line, may lead to upheaval in the ranks (Paynich 2003).

However, although technical skills are necessary, they are not the central elements of readiness for e-learning. Independence, autonomy, and self-direction in learning are even more important (Piskurich 2003, 92). Ultimately, learners can only be taught if they are motivated and are willing to learn (Goldwasser 2001).

For employees who don't have Internet access in their work areas, Kodak has set up more than 150 learning centers and walk-up computers throughout its facilities worldwide (Stim 2002). Each Home Depot store has at least two e-learning computers solely dedicated to the training function. The training is tracked through Home Depot's homegrown learning-management system (Sosbe 2002a).

Employees at Braxton can access the learning channel through their intranet portal where they can find thousands of online courses that are developed internally and by vendors. The portal has direct links to live synchronous training, simulations, online self-study guides, videos, PowerPoint presentations, e-mail, and white papers. The learning management system centralizes the administrative functions such as registration and tracking of each individual's learning progress (Gold 2003). At General Motors University Online, 88,000 managerial, professional, and technical employees can create individual development plans, track their individual training histories, and use e-learning to align their training with development plans in various functional areas of the company (Pantazis 2002). Electronic performance support systems serve as a repository of corporate knowledge, including policies and procedures. The systems give employees a knowledge-management system that centralizes information. (Hassett 2002). IBM and Microsoft use e-learning to offer specialized graduate-level courses to employees seeking advanced degrees. The two corporations will sponsor employees who take courses from home in the evenings and on weekends, capitalizing on the flexibility of e-learning (Goodridge 2002).

In addition to providing the technical support that learners need, corporations should provide an incentive, because desired behavior should be rewarded (Piskurich, 2003, 109). The learner should perceive some tangible benefit, which may mean qualifying for better job prospects or higher salary (Page 2005). At Skandia, cash awards and certificates are given in recognition of completion of various programs. Employees get a cash bonus of $100 if they finish the modules for a certificate program. They also receive diplomas from American Skandia University, which they proudly display (McConnell 2002). If you make a course mandatory for pay raise or promotion, the number of people who take the course will substantially increase (Lovelace 2003). However, if a program is mandatory, it should be done carefully so as not to discourage learners from choosing optional courses in the future (Beamish et al. 2002). Accountability will enhance learner participation. Wachovia Securities provides employee transcripts to managers. Knowing that their managers will consider continuing education in their performance reviews is a powerful incentive for learners (McConnell 2002).

Supporting Instructors

E-learning is driving more firms to focus on training and trainers. Teaching e-learning can be more difficult than teaching in a classroom. Instructors will need to learn how to teach in an e-learning environment. Corporation must also assuage instructors' fears that e-learning will empty out the classroom (Rosenberg 2001, 239). Phillips and Pope discussed a program that is designed to teach instructors to use Web technology to serve employees' professional development needs. It incorporates online learning case studies to help trainers address important business issues, including cost benefits and ROI (Phillips and Pope 2001). The Internet has blurred the line between who is the content user and who is the content provider. Gayeski of ISD said that e-learning is collaborative sharing of knowledge, and in a new training environment, some participants might be the content experts in addressing emerging information (Galagan 2000). However, trainers should still be proactive, conduct needs assessments, embrace technology, and understand the business (Caudron 2001). They can assist in selecting online programs that meet companies' goals and standards (Dobbs 2000a).

Corporate Support

Organizations that have strong values regarding learning and performance improvement are typically the ones that have the support resources necessary to institute e-learning in the workplace. An organization's cultures and its leaders are reflections of each other. Building a culture that will embrace e-learning means building senior management support for that culture (Rosenberg 2001, 189–193).

Edgar Schein, a well-known social psychologist and sociologist from Harvard, said that culture is developed when a group has enough common experience and sufficient shared history. Culture is defined as the end product of norms and behaviors that are supported and rewarded over many years. According to Schein, "Culture matters because it is a powerful latent and often unconscious set of forces that determine both our individual and collective behavior, ways of perceiving, thought patterns, and values. Organizational culture in particular matters because cultural elements determine strategy, goals, and modes of operation" (Schein 1999, 13–14).

IBM calls its training operation "learning services," which sends a strong signal about its commitment to e-learning (Billington 2003). Ted Hoff, Chief Learning Officer, said, "learning is the core DNA of IBM. It is fundamental to our heritage and our culture and our future" (Hoff 2002).

Managers may have good intentions to support e-learning but, in terms of immediate ROI, it can compare unfavorably to being on the road selling to customers (Ettinger 2005). However, without corporate support, it is doubtful that an e-learning initiative will succeed. Leaders who understand and support the e-learning team to provide the best solutions are important in the success of e-learning (Waight and Stewart 2005). Corporate support is particularly important during economic downturns when funding is scarce. Therefore, securing initial buy-in is not enough. Commitment on a continual basis in good times and bad is equally important (Hassett 2002).

Learning Management System

Learning management systems (LMS) are used for tracking e-learning enrollments, maintaining course catalogues and assessing learners' skills.

Learning management systems contain management information on knowledge, skills, and competency profiles, and they can match a profile with an employee's skills to determine training required (Beamish et al. 2002). Learning management systems at GE track training and scheduling of over 300,000 employees (Marsan 2003). Verizon's centralized LMS offers more than 1,200 courses to more than 170,000 employees. Learning management system implementation requires availability of bandwidth, technical staff, support, and a partnership with service and product providers (NETg 2002). Technology can play a big role in e-learning activities by making centralized management and measurements possible (Oakes 2003c).

Technical standards for content development and content sharing enable different programs from different vendors to work together on a common platform. The Department of Defense with academia, the private sector, and the technology sector has developed standards for interoperability known as the Sharable Courseware Object Reference Model (SCORM) (Piskurich 2003). At Braxton, IT, learning technologies, and infrastructures worked with many content providers to make sure their products were compatible with the learning management and other systems in the company. Braxton's IT department needed to become knowledgeable in interoperability standards to help vendors understand the company's SCORM needs. Braxton started by tracking completions. They worked with content providers to track usage of everything from self-paced content to virtual classes to downloadable content. They wanted their employees to be able to go to the learning catalogue, get updated information on a particular technology, complete it in 15 minutes, and then go back to the client with the information (Gold 2003).

Corporations with separate LMS systems (manufacturing and customer service systems) find that systems don't communicate with each other. It is better to treat LMS as a part of the large-scale information system that serves as a single point of entry (Sparta 2002).

How Is Effectiveness Determined by Corporations?

Corporations use customer satisfaction, student competence, improved work processes, and savings as measures of effectiveness. Effectiveness can mean quality or a new way of doing business.

Rationale

No corporation can afford to take a hit-or-miss approach to training, and no corporation can afford training that doesn't have a tangible benefit to the business. Meister of Corporate University Exchange, speaking about e-learning measures, said, "Corporate educators need to create a whole new set of e-learning measures. They need to measure success by asking people: did they get the information they needed, were they satisfied, and were they an active participant? Quality of e-learning can be created from meaningful feedback which is fostered by openness and collaboration" (Leacock 2005). The success of e-learning is measured by how many people say they would take another e-learning course (Verespej 2001).

To measure learner satisfaction, testing and assessments are an essential part of the process. Tests based on consistent standards provide an objective way to measure the skills and knowledge of the learner. If the goal is to get employees to learn actual job skills that can translate to benefits for the employee and the organization, it is necessary to provide proof of effectiveness (Brannick 2003). One benefit of evaluation is to provide feedback to subject matter experts and content designers so they can improve their decision-making process in e-learning (Hicks 2000). Effectiveness can be improved quality in performance. Xerox Europe Limited, for example, implemented e-learning for training its call-center staff so that they are able to demonstrate professional telephone techniques and strong communication and interpersonal skills. This will allow employees to deal with calls successfully and will enable them to direct the call to the appropriate person (Evans 2002).

The ultimate goal of effective e-learning is to drive business results. Corporate performance can be enhanced through alignment of training and business strategy (Beamish et al. 2002). Managers need to demonstrate that e-learning is having a positive impact on corporate strategy and investment objectives. If the business goal of an e-learning program cannot be identified, then there should be a query on why it is there in the first place. Posner of Cisco Systems said that the five areas of measurement are efficiency (train faster), effectiveness (train to do a better job), cost avoidance (travel expenses), customer satisfaction (customer's perception), and business revolution (radical change in business practice) (Gale 2002).

Soft cost savings that reflect value-added productivity, improved retention, and greater satisfaction are more difficult to measure. The ultimate value of e-learning comes when e-learning is linked to achieving a company's goals (Gale 2002).

Methods of Measurements

In 1959, Donald Kirkpatrick, a management professor at the University of Wisconsin, came up with a training model consisting of four levels of evaluation: Level 1 evaluates the effectiveness perceived by trainee; Level 2 measured evaluation of learning; Level 3 observed performance improvement; Level 4 evaluates business impact such as ROI. Since its advent in 1959, this evaluation model has become an industry standard for training measurement. Although Level 4 results are expensive and difficult to obtain, an online learning initiative is not worth much if it does not lead to measurable business benefits (Goldwasser 2001). E-learning typically will reduce travel expenses and time away from work, but there will be additional costs for trainers, outside vendors, development, production, delivery of the material, hardware, software, and administrative support (Galloway 2005).

Many corporations use the Kirkpatrick framework to measure the success of e-learning (Beamish et al. 2002). NCR deployed a project management program and got a 90 percent completion rate. In addition, 96 percent of those who completed the program enjoyed the program (Kirkpatrick Level 1) and had a passing score of 80 percent or better (Kirkpatrick Level 2). Post-monthly training status reports indicate that Kirkpatrick Level 3 was achieved. NCR will attempt to evaluate the bottom line ROI (Kirkpatrick Level 4) (Goldwasser 2001).

Home Depot compared sales results at stores that had and had not received training. A recent sales training program targeted 125 managers who received training at the New England locations, and all but three managers gave a perfect 5.0 score. Home Depot has a stellar reputation for customer service and making good on commitments to customer service. This requires having educated employees at all levels of the company (Sosbe 2002b).

In addition to Kirkpatrick, Bersin also described a five-step program to measure effectiveness and discussed the required measurements for each of these steps using data from the LMS. The five steps include enrollments, progress, completion, scores, and feedback. Feedback will reveal important information such as quality of content, interactivity, and value of material. The problem with lengthy e-learning training is that most people drop out before they pick up enough knowledge to use it in a meaningful way (Laine 2003). Accurate feedback will alert corporations to potential problems so that they can lower the dropout rate.

Cablevision will track a control group of 100 untrained customer service reps versus those who are getting training at the same time to compare sales performance (Berry 2000). At Rockwell Collins, an e-learning program on manufacturing tasks for one group was compared with another group with classroom training and the results for the two methods were the same (Gale 2002).

However, even if workers don't complete an online course, it can still prove effective. Workers may be able to take away relevant parts that are applicable to their jobs, and they will know where to find that information on line (Lynch 2002). IBM came to the conclusion that learners perceive that real and lasting leadership improvements are directly linked to the training, which drives up financial value for the company (Mantyla 2001). Return on equity (ROE) is an important measure on corporate profitability. Verizon's manager of measurements and evaluation conducts a 15 to 20 minute interview of the vice president accountable for e-learning to determine ROE. Hodges of Verizon estimates ROE based on what is achieved in relation to expectation and then compares that with actual data. Surveys are also done with a control group to link training development with overall corporate performance (Berry 2000).

Nowaski, director of e-learning at Kodak said "We made a determination that the best way to look at our investments was to ask what the cost for classroom training is now, including vendor payments, as well as clerical and other overheads, and what it would take for us to deliver the same or more training in a self-study environment" (Harris 2001).

What Lessons Are Learned?

Failure can occur on 3 levels: (1) the learner level (learners are poorly prepared, lack motivation or time), (2) the product level, and (3) the organization level (low managerial support, lack of reward structure).

Failure at the Learner Level

Learners may object to e-learning because technology may alarm them (King 2001). Therefore, preparing employees for e-learning is an important step when trying to avoid failure. This means not only knowing the technology but also embracing the mindset learners need in order to take charge of their own learning. E-learning creates a new learning environment around technology. It is not used as a way to complement instructor-led approach, but instead it is used for things that are best done with technology, such as rapid delivery and broad reach (Galagan 2000). E-learning is about tending to employees' need rather than pushing information at employees. Unlike trainees in classroom training, e-learners are not directly accountable to an instructor. E-learning requires self-motivation. Although e-learning is available at any time and any place, it tends to be postponed or not done at all (Weaver 2002). Classroom training that is assigned a given time and place forces learners to attend. It is unrealistic to expect busy people to be motivated to learn at their desks with their discretionary time. Learners must be supported with dedicated time (Honey 2001). In addition, to realize the broader impact of training, an organization has to go beyond measuring only dollars spent or number of hours of training provided. Experts now suggest that organizations should also measure such factors as time to competence, performance gaps eliminated, and strategic skills needed relative to existing skills. Ultimately, organizations are competitive because of their most important asset, their people. The question is not if, but when and how the employees' skills and abilities are developed. It is paramount to present and future growth (Sung 2003).

Learners fail when they expect e-learning to be the same as classroom learning, attempt to fit it in whenever they can without structured schedules, don't actively participate, and don't ask for help (Broadbent 2000).

E-learning succeeds when it is available when learners want it, when it helps them improve on what they need to do, and when they actually have the desire to do it. If trainees become disillusioned from a bad experience, it is very difficult to rekindle their interests (Waller 2001).

Failure at the Product Level

At the product level, weak content, poorly blended components, lack of alignment with learner or business needs, and lack of time or place for training can lead to failure of learning objectives (Weaver 2002).

Ignoring content can lead to failure. Content must be relevant and cannot be treated as a commodity. It is not one size fits all; it must be tailored to the specific needs of the audience. Content must be learned knowledge that can impart skills and be applied. Employees learn about their organization's values by applying those values in realistic simulated situations, not by reading about them. For example, new hires' orientation can be presented through learning-by-doing activities and by learning valuable and complex lessons from simulations in which there are realistic consequences that unravel, based on decisions new hires make, rather than on clear-cut answers. E-learning can also function well as pretraining to be undertaken before learners attend classroom training so they have a shared point of reference in their simulated experience (Schank 2002, 37).

Designers fail when they don't consult stakeholders, don't pay any attention to create learning, don't test training material, and are too enamored with technology (Broadbent 2000). Design should connect e-learning to existing job processes and systems. It should capture the actual conditions under which learners will access and use the e-learning solutions (Cone and Robinson 2001).

Prior to designing or implementing an e-learning solution, e-learning professionals should assess readiness of the work environment to support the new or improved skills. They should make sure enrollment systems used by learners are comparable to traditional programs. The systems should have prerequisites or requirements for attendance that are comparable to those for traditional programs, and they should develop a method to indicate to managers that their staffs have completed the program or module. They should also monitor participants to determine whether they are applying what they learned (Cone and Robinson 2001). Systems should develop an ongoing feedback loop, make sure learners are compatible with e-learning and develop a competitive analysis to show the benefit of e-learning (Berry 2000).

Ignoring technology can also lead to failure at the product level. Operating systems, Web browsers, tracking systems, LMS, and database and video servers are required to deliver content, but fixating too much on technology can lead to failure. Dow Chemicals' first customer-relationship management strategy turned out to be a costly venture because it focused too much on technology rather than tying in corporate strategy with people's day-to-day operations (Henry 2001). E-learning is not just about technology—it is about learners and what they learn. It's about relevant content delivered in the most technically feasible and user-friendly way. This may mean building a Web system adaptable to the lowest technical specifications a user might require (Schank 2002).

E-learning should be tailored to fit the needs of the individual and integrated into the individual's work; it should use technology that makes it possible to customize and personalize content and delivery to match individual learning styles, experience, and skills; and it should keep learners at pace with the speed of change in business (Pantazis 2002).

Failure at the Organizational Level

At the organizational level, lack of leadership, lack of management support, lack of organizational value placed on learning, and poor marketing can lead to failure of learning goals (Weaver 2002).

Many efforts often overlook the complexities of the interactions between e-learning and the organization and how difficult it is to change people's attitude about e-learning. With so many business variables and interested parties involved, a more strategic approach is necessary to ensure that e-learning has the best possible chance to succeed. A true e-learning strategy certainly addresses technology and learning effectiveness, but it also addresses issues of culture, leadership, justification, organization, talent, and change (Rosenberg 2001).

The notion that just implementing e-learning will automatically draw employees to it is a misconception. Corporate support is needed to combat failure at the organizational level. Cultural resistance does exist where local managers don't treat e-learning as a serious training activity and don't give employees time to learn (Beamish et al. 2002). As a result, poor learner satisfaction and indisposition of learners to use e-learning occurs (Lytras, Pouloudi, and Poulymenakou 2002).

E-learning should be integrated with the workflow and culture of the organizations. The leader and learner must see e-learning as a part of the company's strategy. Success requires leadership, coaching, a supportive work environment, and learner motivation (Piskurich 2003). Administrators fail when they hand off everything to external consultants, don't communicate, use off-the-shelf solutions only, and don't plan for an evaluation (Broadbent 2000).

Input should be solicited from managers and program participants. E-learning professionals should meet with the manager to agree on actions that management must take to address identified barriers to skills transfer. They should resist the manager's request to provide an e-learning solution when the work environment won't support skills transfer (Cone and Robinson 2001).

Lack of managerial support, interruptions at the workplace, unpleasant prior e-learning experiences, and high investments for technological developments are obstacles to e-learning (Beamish et al. 2002). Executive buy-in and support mechanisms such as mentoring, coaching, online library and Web resources are needed to overcome workplace barriers (Ingram Sandelands, and Teare 2001).

Failure to involve IT can also prove problematic. This group's involvement is important because IT ensures that the computing environment is functioning and secure. (Weaver 2002). IT is valuable in developing and maintaining software and technology. Partnering early with the IT department is a key to success (Gold 2003).

Organizational support means understanding the level of commitment and investment involved in e-learning. Preparing content and courseware requires substantial costs for planning, infrastructure, bandwidth, system integration, and communication (Weaver 2002).

The success of e-learning requires corporate commitment that is equal to other mission-critical initiatives. It is important to know what the goal is and what is to be achieved. The goal could support a specific corporate initiative; streamline training; increase skills; lower costs; and support field force, customers, or distribution partners. Successful e-learning requires a holistic or integrated approach. It is not about content, delivery, or LMS systems viewed in isolation. It's about how all these elements are integrated, how it is launched, and how it is managed. Employee resistance can be substantial, especially if an organization does not support change or technology implementation. E-learning needs to be compelling to the learners, and it must appeal to them and prove valuable to their career goals and aspirations (Henry 2001).

Dobbs offered an agenda for improving e-learning: (1) stop pretending that reading is training, (2) increase bandwidth, (3) adopt interoperability standards, and (4) conduct internal and external evaluations of Web-based training (Dobbs 2000b). Ultimately, success in e-learning requires a careful balance of technology and needs of e-learners and those who support them (Beamish et al. 2002).

3

FRAMEWORK AND METHODS

Conceptual Framework

The conceptual framework of this study is to investigate how e-learning is developed, implemented, and evaluated in corporations. The primary focus of this research explores in depth how e-learning is created at IBM. In my analysis of e-learning at IBM, I refer to other corporations' e-learning experiences for comparative purposes.

Methodology

This study began with a careful search of well-crafted questions. Numerous iterations were done because of the importance of asking the right questions. Formulating questions precisely is a significant step to facilitate a design with a greater likelihood of successful answers (Light, Singer, and Willet, 1990, 13). Data gathering for this qualitative inquiry was done through a combination of methods. Interviews were my primary method for data collection. These interviews were supplemented with my observations and reviews of documents that interviewees made available to me. In the interpretative study, interviews can be the sole basis of a study, or they can be used in conjunction with data from participant observations and documents (Glesne & Peshkin, 1992, 64). Major themes are extracted by analyzing interviews and available data. This qualitative study is exploratory in nature. This means that not much literature has been written about the topic or the target population, and the researcher is seeking to learn from the participants and then build an understanding based on their ideas (Creswell 2003, 30). I have analyzed input received from interviewees and have described these findings from the analysis.

Interviews

The fieldwork relied primarily on interviews. These contacts were made possible from my current business associations with IBM and other corporations. Gaining access came from their trust in working with Con Edison and the assurance that information from interviewees would not be used competitively or in a manner that would damage their companies. IBM has sales and technical support people that frequently visit Con Edison's headquarters in New York City. Interviews were conducted with professionals who are involved in e-learning. These include the chief learning officers, human resources personnel, content developers, designers, technologists, instructors, administrative support personnel, learners, and various mangers. A set of protocols or questions was posed to interviewees to understand how e-learning is developed, how e-learning is balanced with traditional face-to-face training, how corporations implement and support e-learning, and how corporations determine if e-learning is effective as a tool for learning. The determination of effectiveness was made from the interviewees' perspectives about how they define and measure effectiveness.

Protocol

Key questions and the subset questions are enumerated below.

Why Use E-Learning?
- What is the strategic reason for using it?
- What is the role of technology in e-learning?
- How do size, geography, and speed come in to play?
- What is the role of accessibility?
- What is the expectation on investment and productivity?

How Is E-Learning Developed?
- How do you select content and design for e-learning?
- How do you build work practice into e-learning?
- How do you consider the target audience?
- How do you build collaboration and interactivity into e-learning?

- How do you balance classroom training and e-learning?
- How do you determine how to deliver the content to target audiences?
- How do you decide what technology to use?
- Who are all the professionals involved in the development?
- Who develops e-learning?
- Do you develop it internally, in partnership with others, or do you outsource?

How Is E-Learning Implemented?

- How do you make sure that e-learning will be accepted?
- What type of corporate support is required?
- How do you describe your learning culture?
- How do you bring about culture change?
- How do you prepare instructors?
- How do you support the learners?
- How do you market e-learning?
- How do you launch e-learning?
- How do you keep track of the learners' progress?

How Is Effectiveness Determined?

- What are your criteria for evaluating e-learning?
- What types of measurements do you use?
- What are the difficulties in measuring effectiveness?
- What is the feedback from learners, instructors, and managers?
- How does e-learning change the way you do business?

What Lessons Are Learned?

- What problems are encountered on the learner side?
- What problems are encountered with e-learning products?
- What cultural hurdles are encountered?
- What problems with corporate support are encountered?
- What are difficult areas to apply e-learning and why?
- What technology hurdles are encountered?

I generally started by giving the interviewees an overall scope of what I am trying to accomplish so that they can have a sense of where their particular area of expertise will fit into the overall framework. I posed the same protocol to all interviewees but focused more in the area of each person's expertise. For example, a facilitator knows more about instruction and interaction with learners than about evaluating the rate of ROI. A content designer knows more about interaction with the subject-matter expert and how best to convey the course material to learners. An administrator is more familiar with tracking of e-learning activities and making sure learners are making the right amount of progress. I tried to be sensitive to areas that e-learning professionals are unable to respond to and just moved on quickly. I honed in on areas that they knew well and explored those in depth. I interviewed numerous e-learning professionals and managers. The exact number of people to be interviewed was not as critical as the need to make sure that the research questions were answered by a sufficient range of e-learning professionals. The number of interviewees for each company varied to some degree based on the principal players in each of the three companies that were involved in various aspects of e-learning. My preferred method was to do in-person interviews. If that was not feasible in some cases, telephone interviews were the alternative. For the most part, I was able to do in-person interviews.

I made observations and was a participant in selected e-learning programs such as the Basic Blue program for managers at IBM. Interviews were conducted at corporate and satellite locations. Qualitative research should be done at the natural setting, and that means research should be done at the home or office of the participants (Creswell, 2003, 181). I visited IBM's chief learning officer, chief e-learning officer, instructors, and trainees at the IBM learning center in Armonk, New York. I visited e-learning professional such as chief learning officer, chief information officer, technologist, instructor, human resources manger, content designers, technologists, and trainers in other corporations. I taped all the interviews and informed and obtained consent from the interviewees beforehand. Interviews generally ran between one to one and one-half hours. Information from one interview was used to ask questions to subsequent people. Notes were transcribed shortly after the interviews. Internal documents, memos, and videotapes provided to me were examined. Multiple interviews were done at each company and open-ended questions were asked. I interpreted interview transcripts, observation notes, documents, and videos. Observations included taking notes on the surroundings and the attitudes and body language of the e-learning professionals and learners during my visits at their locations. I looked for the uniqueness of their learning environment, such as equipment availability, space, and time for learning. I also looked for their level of comfort with e-learning and their level of enthusiasm. I tried to see if there was a relationship between learning and having a supportive learning environment. The lessons learned from IBM and other corporations' e-learning programs would serve as a guide for other corporations.

Data Recording Procedure

A detailed running log was kept. This included a detailed account of all interview and data-collection activities. Qualitative research typically relies on four methods of collecting information: participation, observation, in-depth interviews and analysis of documents (Marshall and Rossman, 1999, 105). Recorded interviews were immediately transcribed and reviewed. Notes from these interviews were immediately typed. In addition to interviews, raw data, tapes, and other documents were made available to me. Data analysis (field notes, interviews, document summaries), data synthesis, description and analytic memos, and notes on methodological decisions and trustworthiness criteria were also included. The strengths and weaknesses of each type of data were noted. Observation protocol included demographic information such as time, place, date, and setting. Descriptive notes included interviewees, dialogue, physical settings, and reflective notes including personal thoughts, impressions, speculations, and feelings. Interview protocol for recording information includes a heading, opening statement, research questions, follow-up questions, and space for recording comments and reflections. The medium for recording included handwritten notes and audiotapes. Recorded documents indicated primary information received directly from people under study or a secondary source from reports and documents.

Data Analysis and Interpretation

Data analysis is the process of bringing order, structure, and interpretation to the mass of collected data (Marshall and Rossman, 1999, p. 130). Qualitative data analysis is research for general statements about relationships among categories of data; it builds grounded theory (Strauss and Corbin, 1990).

When data from interviews, notes, and documents were gathered, these data were organized for further analysis. The process began with coding of the interview material by major themes, ideas, and concepts (Rubin and Rubin, 1995, 238). The coding process was a way to generate a description of the setting or people as well as themes for further analysis. The coding and organization of data was a process of reflection on an ongoing basis. After completing each interview, the examination of the data identified themes that described the world of the interviewees and indicated areas that should be examined in more detail (Rubin and Rubin, 1995, 226). The data were categorized into why e-learning is used, how e-learning is developed, how e-learning is implemented, and how e-learning is evaluated. Review of all the data provided a general sense of what the overall finding was. This included the determination of whether these themes could be integrated into a coherent storyline and whether there was a close nexus between development and implementation and how they impact e-learning effectiveness. The description and themes could be represented in a qualitative narrative and a theory could be developed. This represented a set of concepts or themes and the proposed relationships among them (Maxwell 1996).

Qualitative studies are also subject to research traps. For example, interviews can make it seem like there is a large amount of evidence being gathered, but unless a sufficient range of opinion is sought, the evidence might be inadequate or quite unreliable. By interviewing many people in each of these companies and interviewing them separately, confirming and disconfirming views on various issues were captured, and this enhanced the trustworthiness of the findings. I took care to avoid major types of evidentiary flaws including inadequate amount of evidence; inadequate variety in kinds of evidence to warrant key assertions; failure to triangulate; failure to engage in member check (which means going back to the participants and asking them if this makes sense); faulty interpretive status of evidence that was either misunderstood or misleading; inadequate collection of disconfirming information, or different opinions or multiple ways of interpreting the same data; and inadequate discrepant case analysis (Erikson 1986, 140–141).

Trustworthiness

Multiple means were used to ensure that data are trustworthy. Interviewing numerous experts from each of the three companies enhanced trustworthiness. Triangulation, discussions with different people, and framing questions to remove possible bias were done. This study is rich in descriptions to convey findings. Any personal bias is identified and declared. Opposing views to the themes were actively solicited. I spent prolonged time in interviewee locations (Creswell 2003, 196). Interviewees were asked to review this study for accuracy and to confirm the validity of findings. Peer reviews were also conducted. Peers were consulted about how best to present sensitive information. This research offers findings that others can use as a reference for e-learning.

Ethical Considerations

This was not backyard research, but nonetheless, precaution was taken to make sure it was not biased. Although IBM supplies products and services to Con Edison, my employer, Con Edison is not a competitor in the e-learning business. Con Edison currently does not use much e-learning. Permission was granted by interviewees to tape record these interviews. Interviewees were also given the opportunity to review this study. This review by participants served as a way to ensure accuracy and as a way to confirm trustworthiness. I adhered to the basic ethical principles of minimizing the burden and keeping the participant as informed as possible about the research (Erikson, 1986, 119). Interviews were done at the time and place of interviewees' convenience. Recording observations and interviews did not intrude excessively in the ongoing flow of daily events (Marshall and Rossman, 1999, 148).

4

IBM

This description of how e-learning is created is based on numerous interviews of key e-learning professionals at IBM. It also includes literature search and a review of internal documents.

Ted Hoff, who is the chief learning officer, was hired by the former CEO Lou Gerstner several years ago to unify IBM's learning community. At that time, training had been fragmented, and the sheer size of the company clearly called for someone to oversee activities of the entire learning community at IBM. The unifying effort was undertaken through a close cooperation between the chief learning officer's learning leaders and business organizations through a strategic learning-plan process. The chief learning officer named a learning leader for each of the major businesses in the company. These learning leaders work closely with their respective businesses, such as global services, technology, software, sales, and distribution, to assess their learning requirements and recommend learning solutions.

Under Hoff's leadership, e-learning has increased dramatically to 48 percent of all learning at IBM. In a personal interview in 2004, Hoff said, "We do e-business. We want to promote e-learning. I am personally now taking a different angle. It's not the percentage of e-learning that's the goal. It's the caliber."

Why Use E-Learning?

Efficiency, cost savings, the ability to reach a global community and to be in the forefront of technology and innovative use of technology are the key considerations for using e-learning at IBM. First, substantial savings result from avoided travel and associated expenses. The extra time that it takes to go to a classroom setting is time lost, and that also converts into additional revenues. It is estimated that IBM achieves $400 million in annual savings by using e-learning, e-meetings, and instant messaging (Adkins 2003). In addition to benefiting IBM, e-learning also offers convenience to learners.

In some circumstances, however, classroom learning may be more appropriate. John Wattendorf, a content expert, explained in a personal interview in 2004, "We tried to take a look at the cognitive domain and ask ourselves if any of the learning seem to be in the lower level of the cognitive domain. We wanted to try to move that out of the face-to-face type of workshop because it's really not the best way to spend people's time and because it cost so much. We want to optimize their face-to-face time." Matt McLaughlin, a learning leader in the sales and distribution business unit, said, "Not everything can be done via e-learning. It has its place." When training sellers to close major deals worth hundreds of million dollars, they use e-learning as a prerequisite, followed by three in-person workshops spread over the course of about a six-month period. Each workshop is three and one-half days in duration, and in between workshops, they assign a mentor and a coach to every participant to help them apply the learning to real-life opportunities that they're working on (McLaughlin, personal interview, 2004).

When e-learning is being applied, it must be relevant and focused for the target audience. Hoff explained that the idea of indiscriminately having massive numbers of courses up on a Web site that people could tap into doesn't work. "Having a lot of courses on the Web doesn't mean that we are doing anything for anybody that's really valuable. People realized that that was not effective learning," said Hoff in a personal interview in 2004. Effective e-learning comes from experience. At IBM, people are using a lot of e-learning when developing their own programs for their own needs. In this process, they learn how to make e-learning work.

Serve the Global Community

E-learning provides the ability to facilitate learning in a global community. The important context is that IBM is a huge global company with 315,000 people doing business in 178 countries. Hoff said "We have a natural need to try to figure out how to develop people and align people in a global rapid way and that lends itself to try to figure out how to do things not face-to-face, but over the Web and network" (Hoff, personal interview, 2004). Teresa Golden, vice president of marketing added, "Because 40 percent of our employees are mobile in any point and time, trying to pull all these people into central locations to get trained simply wasn't going to work. So we had to leverage technology in order to address some of those issues" (Golden, personal interview, 2004).

Technology Innovation—On Demand Learning

IBM is a premier technology company, so there is a natural desire to always try to be at the leading edge in developing technology and using it in a creative way. Hoff explained, "IBM, for 20 years, because of the nature of our business, was creating various kinds of network applications. IBM has a very natural interest in seeing how far we can go with e-learning. The company has been pioneering in this field, part of this natural extension of what we have been doing for decades" (Hoff, personal interview, 2004).

A case in point in driving technological innovation is IBM's latest e-learning strategy called On Demand Learning. The concept is simple but the implication can be quite significant. The idea behind on-demand is to bring learning to the learner at the desktop. The underlying principle is that, in the computer age, employees should be getting the learning material continuously rather than attending isolated modules. Learning is brought immediately to the workplace, which is very different from the traditional way of going to a class and registering for a course. On-demand learning addresses the challenges that a person faces everyday and provides a tool to solve those particular problems. Lau explained, "Say you're over budget in this area. How can you get cost saving to offset that kind of problem? So then there's some learning material that shows some best practices in the past you might want to think about. And that kind of learning is constructed in a way that's just in time for you and that basically is on-demand learning." On-demand learning can be more effective than doing simulations in a lab. Lau explained, "Simulation is like a cockpit. You go into pilot training. That means risk free even though you failed in flying a 747. But it is not a real situation" (Lau, personal interview, 2004).

On-demand learning has potential implications in other facets of operation. Wattendorf explained, "What are the implications for leaders in the on-demand world? Does that mean something different and how

IBM can become the best example of an organization that, in all its aspects, is organized to achieve success in the on-demand world. It's not just strategy vis-à-vis our customers, but it's how we work internally as well" (Wattendorf, personal interview, 2004). Chak Lau added, "The goal of learning is to have the highest impact on business and we want to link that to IBM's On Demand Learning. Basically learning is not just a transitional activity but rather it's a continuum, it's a journey" (Lau, personal interview, 2004). Teresa Golden said, "In today's world what people really want is just-in-time learning as opposed to just-in-case learning. So they need the information to solve a specific task that they're working on right then and there" (Golden, personal interview, 2004).

How Is E-Learning Developed?

Learning Organization Structure

The chief learning officer has a staff of 136 people who report to him directly, but in addition, all training personnel within businesses report to him on a dotted-line basis. He provides guidance to the global learning structure that spans across Europe, Asia, Canada, and South America. The chief learning officer's corporate staff has expertise in design, development, and delivery of e-learning. He provides guidance, but the businesses for the most part run their own training in areas that are unique to them. Accordingly, funding for training mostly resides locally with individual businesses. The chief learning officer hosts a monthly call with 700 learning professionals from the entire learning community to discuss priority initiatives, strategic directions of the businesses, and issues pertinent to the global learning community (Zinzi, personal interview, 2004). He also meets with business executives periodically to focus on what learning solutions will help the businesses achieve their goals and to emphasize IBM's high priority for learning.

The chief learning officer's corporate-learning organization sponsors a limited number of programs with a particular emphasis on leadership training for executives. Basic Blue is IBM's signature program on leadership development. It is well known throughout the industry as a premier management training program. Basic Blue has an enterprise-wide focus and is used to train more than 30,000 IBM managers worldwide (Zinzi, personal interview, 2004).

Business Objectives

Defining business objectives, assembling the right team, assigning responsibilities, and taking a practical and cost efficient approach are some of the ingredients necessary in developing e-learning at IBM. According to Hoff, the decision- making process for all learning starts with the business perspective. That is, what are people trying to accomplish, how are they trying to build their organization, and what's the role of learning in enabling people to build their workforce, capability, organization, and business (Hoff, personal interview, 2004). The learning leader will get input from the subject-matter expert and the designer to decide how best to design the curriculum and how best to leverage e-learning. IBM tries to build upon what's already available and systematically incorporate feedback on lessons learned. Hoff explained, "Because we have done a lot of e-learning, we also look at how we can do two very important things. First, how can we use existing approaches, so that we don't have to spend a lot of money to create new learning programs? Second, how can we reuse existing approaches so that the learning that we are providing is now integrated into people's work?" For example, for training a sales manager, IBM has now integrated sales, industry knowledge, and management training together into a single program (Hoff, personal interview, 2004).

On a daily basis, the learning leaders are involved with their respective business leaders side-by-side to understand their business strategy, objectives, goals, skill requirements, and how learning can play a part in that process. They will meet with senior executives, help them identify priorities, and offer them business solutions that will provide the most business impact (Arrington, personal interview, 2004). The chief learning officer will review business requirements with learning leaders and will extract those requirements that are common among businesses. When this occurs, the chief learning officer will pool resources and work on the basis of an enterprise-wide initiative that adds value to multiple businesses in the most efficient way (Zinzi, personal interview, 2004).

Project Management—Collaborative Effort

Developing e-learning is a project-management process. There is a deployment plan and a target schedule set for the project team. The principal players are in regular communication and everyone understands his or her piece of the development and design. Each step of the schedule is monitored.

It's a plan that covers every point, from the beginning when the requirements are set to the point of delivery. It is a collaborative effort involving a number of different types of learning and technical professionals. The learning leader initially assesses what types of learning solutions should be used for an initiative and whether it should be an e-learning, classroom, or a blended approach but the principal decision maker is the owner of the initiative (Arrington, personal interview, 2004). This is usually owned by the business that is sponsoring the initiative. The owner is the final decision maker about whether the business will fund the learning project. For example, the management development group under the chief learning officer owns the Basic Blue program. It funds the program and is the final arbiter on content, design, and delivery. The designer's role is to offer new ideas and create options. Technical experts are responsible for digitizing the content. However, the owner is the final decision maker. To illustrate the role of different expertise, Wattendorf, a content provider and designer, explained, "We don't do the technology piece. For example, when we're developing what we wanted in "edvisor", a leadership development tool, I wrote the logic behind edvisor, but I don't do any of the programming. Then I turn that over to one of our technology experts, and we've also got people that are very skilled in the appropriate look and feel of Web site"(Wattendorf, personal interview, 2004). The owner is generally the project manager. Bob MacGregor, who is the owner of the Basic Blue program, explained, "I own the content, I own the delivery and the deployment of the program. I work with the designers who come up with the design concept but I'm the final arbiter. I work with the technologists who could do this great videotape, but I'm the one who's going to make the decision to deploy it or not" (MacGregor, personal interview, 2004). About teamwork, Hoff proudly said, "This is one of my most proud personal accomplishments. I think that the teamwork is very strong now. There was always teamwork, but the processes weren't defined as to who owns content, design, and delivery. IBM operates off a matrix system, so we have to make it work. We have to get things done with other people that don't work for you" (Hoff, personal interview, 2004).

Sequence of Participation

According to Beverly Sanford, a learning partner, when deciding when to bring various people on the project-management team into the process, the answer varies depending on the nature of the project. The sequence of events will change from project to project. Sanford explained in a 2004 personal interview, "There are times when I may work in parallel. There are times when things are more sequential. I may bring a learning consultant in from the very beginning as I'm working on the requirements, if I feel that they're pretty complex. I may wait and gather the requirements myself and bring a learning consultant in after the requirements have been defined."

E-Learning versus Classroom Learning

Blended learning is taking the best features of classroom learning and e-learning and combining them into a blended approach. However, it's not always clear how best to balance the two components. Not every application is suitable for e-learning. When asked about what is the right balance, Hoff said, "E-learning is an extension of e-business. We want to create it where it's effective. We want to have a bias toward using e-learning to ensure that if something has to be done face-to-face, we will absolutely do it. But since face-to-face is so critical and expensive, we will try to do it in a blended way, leveraging e-learning with the face-to-face effort" (Hoff, personal interview, 2004). But the e-learning piece is becoming more pervasive. IBM's On Demand Strategy is one such example. Under this strategy, the new workplace has learning embedded in every employee's workstation and gives each employee full access that cuts across computer platforms to get what he or she needs, when he or she needs it (Arrington, personal interview, 2004).

IBM is constantly experimenting with e-learning to find out where it is most applicable as a learning tool. It's a matter of knowing when it makes sense to use it. IBM uses a very systematic approach. They use a four-tier model called The E-Learning Model to determine what should appropriately be e-learning. The first tier covers information and awareness. The second tier covers understanding of work practices. The third tier involves collaborative learning through simulations. The fourth tier is the face-to-face intervention (Sloman 2002, 46). Content that fall within the first three tiers are done online, whereas the fourth tier is reserved for a classroom interactive session.

Content/Design

Subject Matter Experts (SME)

Subject matter experts are needed to make sure the content is relevant and up to date. Learners should be learning things that are relevant to their workplace performance. Learning leaders work with subject-matter experts and designers. For example, if it's a financial program, finance experts will work with the designer on content and design. The designer makes recommendations on delivery and on the tools and resources required. Arrington said, "It's very rare for subject matter experts not to be involved" (Arrington, personal interview, 2004). John Wattendorf, a subject-matter expert, explained, "IBM brought me on board and what I've primarily been responsible for is content expertise in the area of leadership development, and I've done an extensive amount of work in curriculum and course design. I've been a principal designer of several different initiatives. The one that first started using e-learning in a very deliberate and informed way was one that we call Basic Blue" (Wattendorf, personal interview, 2004).

Designers

There is a central design group reporting to the chief learning officer that is responsible for design and development for major enterprise-wide learning projects. If it's an innovative e-learning approach, the central group will take on the project directly. For standard e-learning, it will be handled by other organizations or outside vendors (Lewis, personal interview, 2004). According to Lau, designers and content experts work hand-in-hand to design the best sequence of the content so that it's easily absorbed as well as easily applied. So the designer is accountable for understanding how the knowledge operation can be transferred from the design, through the learning material, to the learner in the best way. Lau explained, "There is a lot of learning psychology, a lot of teaching psychology behind it so that the material is formatted and presented in a way that appeals to all five senses. But you let them learn the best way they can. If the material is presented in too difficult a manner, they just give up. So the motivational level is reduced because the design is never there" (Lau, personal interview, 2004).

Content

The content must be relevant and the context must be appropriate. IBM and many companies initially started off by buying a large library of courses. It had thousands of courses on the Web but a lot of people weren't using them. Hoff explained, "There is no mystery to me why people weren't using it, because the context wasn't right for the job and company. The time wasn't being set aside for anyone to engage in it. No one was following up about whether you used it or not. So you have these low take rates."The bottom line is that e-learning has to be put in the context of the job that someone's doing and aimed toward what changes are required. An example of a pure e-learning initiative that works directly to meet what people need is E-business Sales Essentials for the sales force. It is a series of Web lectures on critical value propositions that IBM can provide to its customers. It is way to keep sales people informed in a timely fashion. Hoff said, "We got to get them out so fast, and we don't want the sales people to always go to class, so we put a mandatory process in place by which the salespeople are supposed to draw these Web lectures down, and then we put a certification at the bottom of it to prove that someone has actually gone through it" (Hoff, personal interview, 2004).

Another key consideration is the proper focus about whether it's e-learning or classroom learning. It may be easier for organizations to buy programs than to hire facilitators to train their employees. But if e-learning is done indiscriminately, it can be perceived as learning without focus; it would not be clear to people what's important. Nancy Lewis, vice president of On Demand Learning, explained, "The e-learning piece is always easier to disconnect from than face-to-face."That ability to make motivation inherent is important. It shouldn't be because the manager is forcing the employee to be there. The key is whether it's useful and valuable. "According to Lewis, IBM is frugal at what they add to e-learning. They use top critical things that are key from a business point of view. They also put out there what's fun and engaging" (Lewis, personal interview, 2004).

Repurpose

Repurposing the content means reusing material or content that is valuable for further use. IBM's many initiatives on industry learning solutions involving live conferences were captured for further disseminating to a larger audience. Fran Zinzi, program manager for IBM Learning Organization, said, "We're taking the contents from that and putting it online so we can reach many more. There's no way we could ever afford to send through the numbers [of employees] that we really would like to have this knowledge. We're taking the contents and changing the way we deliver it. So it's not going to classroom. We put it online." For this type of leadership training, it may not be the optimal way, but repurposing is a prudent way of capturing all that learning and knowledge transfer that took place in the classroom. Zinzi said, "We can't send thousands of employees to these classes, but we take the contents and send them into Web lectures online. So we try to do that as much as possible, so that we can reach as many employees who have a need for that knowledge and the skills" (Zinzi, personal interview, 2004).

IBM has also done modularization of content. This is a method to slice content into stand-alone modules. It allows employees to customize courses based on their specific needs (Weintraub, personal interview, 2004).

Cultural Sensitivity

With over 300,000 employees working in different parts of the world, it's a serious challenge to maintain a single culture and yet be sensitive to local needs. IBM has done an excellent job in creating this global learning community. According to Sanford, IBM's basic premise is that they create one global culture, and the creation of learning is designed to meet that need. They will, of course, adapt to local laws as needed. For instance, in India, the Indian learning community will provide guidance because they understand the local laws and regulations. So it may be the same training but the way it is executed may differ based on culture or location. The designers will take cultural implications and the differences in requirements across different geographies into consideration when making appropriate cultural adaptations (Arrington, personal interview, 2004). Golden said, "Some graphics that might be used in an e-learning module in the United States would not be appropriate say, in China. So you have to be very sensitive to those types of issues" (Golden, personal interview, 2004).

Content must also be validated. For example, in leadership training, there is an assessment for competencies. These competencies are validated through analysis of data to make sure that these, in fact, are the behaviors that, if exhibited by a manager, tend to differentiate that manager as a high performer from a typical performer. This would be done on the basis of outcome measures that are focused on meeting business needs. The training will be focused by business units and by individuals (Wattendorf, personal interview, 2004).

Design

According to Wattendorf, design should include good principles for Web writing. It should include ways to make the course interesting and interactive. It should not simply take material that's textual and just put it on the Web.

IBM has experts with PhDs in adult education and experts on use of media to help learning through creative designs. The designers' role is to translate content into something that's appropriate for the Web. For interactivity, simulations are used whenever possible. This provides a means for a person to give a response and then learn from feedback on that response.

Online advisor is another design that helps users. Online advisor serves as a surrogate for a real life advisor when someone is going through an academic program. IBM's online tool, called "edvisor," spelled with an *e* instead of an *a*, is used as a virtual advisor. It's a tool that asks the user a series of questions in order to create a leadership development plan. These questions include, for example, the person's level of experience, skills, and the business context. Edvisor is linked to the feedback from 360 evaluations, so the individual's leadership capabilities can be assessed. It suggests areas in which the employee needs to focus his utmost attention (Wattendorf, personal interview, 2004).

Beta Test

Before a course is rolled out, it's tested with trainers and other potential users. Typically, there is a pilot, and trainers are invited to participate. Their recommendations are carefully reviewed and changes are incorporated if appropriate (Sanford, personal interview, 2004). Arrington added, "Different users come in at the pilot stage, so before our offering or intervention would be made generally available to a wide population, we would first run a test group so that we'll get their feedback" (Arrington, personal interview, 2004).

In the on-demand world, Lewis said that there is a broader implication in design. Lewis explained, "It's understanding the work—it is understanding new possibilities for how to design work. It requires thinking from the workplace environment, thinking from the learner's perspective at work. It's a new way of thinking about e-learning. It's a whole new methodology" (Lewis, personal interview, 2004). According to Lewis, the on-demand strategy brings integration of different functional areas and allows employees to view learning from a totally different perspective. It's an enterprise point of view regarding developing new business. Technology enables IBM to do things that they weren't able to do before. In terms of business models, IBM determined that they had to improve to add value to their customers. To that end, they initiated the On Demand Workplace initiative. This is a total shift in paradigm. Lewis remarked,

"Think about a person actually doing a task at his desktop. And at that very moment, he can be assisted with knowledge and best practices to perform that task" (Lewis, personal interview, 2004).

Learner Consideration

High Touch

According to Lau, everyone needs to have high touch. High touch means interacting with others. If there's no high touch, high tech alone will not work. True, there are some people who simply enjoy programming. They just look at the screen and they are satisfied. But that's a minority. Most people want to talk to people. So, the goal is to figure out how best they can talk to people. Lau said, "It's the young generation that likes the instant messenger (IM). They like to talk to people through technology. The key is to figure out how workers that need high touch can talk to their coworkers, managers, and other learners. What is needed is to build a high-touch element into e-learning" (Lau, personal interview, 2004).

According to Wattenedorf, while IBM is a technology company, not everybody at IBM is necessarily engaged with technology. IBM has the same problems that any company has with e-learning. In response to these problems, there are constant efforts made to make e-learning as easy to use as possible. Wattendorf said, "The user interface is something that's very important to us and creating that in such a way that it's easy to use, that it's intuitive, that the person can do any kind of searches that he wants to" (Wattendorf, personal interview, 2004).

The nature of the audience is a key consideration. Learning leaders will review the target audience and determine requisite skills that may be required. Learning leaders will engage learning consultants and instructional designers to make sure that they come up with the solution that fits the skills and business requirements of the users (Sanford, personal interview, 2004). Designing a solution should consider how comfortable the target audience is with the use of a computer (Arrington, personal interview, 2004).

At times, one size doesn't fit all. If there are unique local needs, they can be accommodated. For example, IBM's greater China group has very young people and is dealing with rapid growth. China's needs are different from those of the United Kingdom, for example, where they have more experience with computers. Therefore, from a global perspective, there are differences in both geography and business units (Wattendorf).

According to Hoff, if e-learning is perceived as a cheap way of doing training, it also will not be well received. Whether someone is comfortable with e-learning may have less to do with age and more to do with whether e-learning is perceived as a lack of learning support from the corporation. It appears that age is not the principal factor. Hoff said, "The principal factor is whether the e-learning is presented in a context where the person perceives it as a cheap alternative to face-to-face learning: Someone saying 'I'm not going to really invest in your development so here's a bunch of Web sites you should go to." The appropriate perception that needs to be conveyed is to make sure that there is a proper job context. Potential users need to be aware that e-learning is an important part of a learning continuum, including a face-to-face session. Hoff said, "Let's do everything over the Web so we can do other important things when we are together" (Hoff, personal interview, 2004).

Delivery

E-learning doesn't always have an instructor. If that's the case, the computer interface where the navigation of the material takes place is an important part of learning facilitation. It would be frustrating to users if it were hard to find out where to go next or to answer the questions or figure out how to turn back. Such navigation designs are integral parts of the delivery vehicle. The navigation must be designed in a way that facilitates learning (Lau, personal interview, 2004).

Blended Learning

IBM's Basic Blue is an excellent example of a blended learning approach. Prior to Basic Blue, the new manager's school was something for participants to go to for a week at the learning center and was a nice time away from business. There were no distractions and participants could really focus on learning. After IBM created Basic Blue, they still had a weeklong session at the learning center, but changed what participants would do when they arrived at the center. In the past, somebody would stand up there showing some slides and that was the coaching model IBM used. But Basic Blue changed all that. IBM began to create different kinds of e-learning that would meet those needs. In Basic Blue, there is a whole suite of modules called "quick views," which give users quick overviews of topics of interest. These could be topics such as conflict resolution, goal setting, performance, and meeting management. Quick views were designed so that a person could get the basic knowledge prior to the face-to-face learning lab. For example, the basics of coaching can be learned online and the opportunity to apply the knowledge could be done when the face-to-face session takes place. Students can actually use their knowledge with real live human beings and get some feedback (Wattendorf, personal interview, 2004).

Basic Blue is designed to train new managers, including those managers who have joined IBM from strategic outsourcing and acquisition. According to Bob MacGregor, Manager of Basic Blue, only about one quarter of new managers is from within IBM, whereas three quarters of the managers come from strategic outsourcing and acquisition each year. These managers come from different companies in different parts of the world and come with different managerial skills. So Basic Blue is designed to accommodate the needs of both of these groups. It is a very important platform to bring managers to a common culture. Thus, what IBM delivers to a management team in the United States is the same as what it delivers in Europe or in Asia or in any other part of the world (MacGregor, personal interview, 2004).

Basic Blue requires participants to do prework through e-learning, then follows up with a week of face-to-face learning lab (Wattendorf, personal interview, 2004). In the e-learning phase, participants can launch from their desktop into IBM's Lotus learning management system. Participants are required to complete a series of modules over a six-month period of time. In the face-to-face session, Basic Blue provides an excellent venue for managers from different parts of the IBM enterprise to learn from each other. It's a tremendous opportunity to learn where they each fit within the large IBM enterprise and to benefit from diversity among managers in terms of experience and discipline. MacGregor said, "The strength of the IBM Company is leveraging the whole IBM Company. We need to make sure that our managers understand the IBM Company more than just their silos. So I may be in software, but I better know what's going on in sales and the other parts of the business. By being here, they get to talk to people from other parts of the business." Diversity is one of IBM's key strengths. Wattendorf remarked, "We try to help them understand the power of diversity, not just necessarily in the EEO sense, not because you might come from a different racial, ethnic, or geographical group, but just the fact that there are differences and that we think differently. That there is a power in bringing together that kind of diversity" (Wattendorf, personal interview, 2004).

Sourcing

IBM will assess the feasibility of buying versus building a program. In most cases, if the standard off-the-shelf library of programs is available, it will be purchased if appropriate. But if a program unique to IBM were necessary, it would be developed internally, particularly if there were no vendors capable of doing the work. For example, all of the designs for Basic Blue were done internally. When IBM began their design work in 1998, there was very little use of e-learning at the time. There were a number of small firms that were doing e-learning, but the vast majority of those programs were done on CD-ROM. They were using a lot of technology including the use of video programs. The challenge IBM had was to go with a proven process that would work globally. Bandwidth was a key issue as some managers in China and elsewhere either could not connect to the Internet or the connection was limited in duration to 10 to 15 minutes. So it was important to recognize that it could take two days for them just to download a single module, which made it impractical.

The other major challenge was that most of the vendors had single country-specific operations and were not equipped to deal with multiple country modules. Some vendors could build software for the United States, and there were a few vendors in other parts of the world that could build software in the country they were in but did not have the capability to create content that would work globally. These vendors could develop content for that single country, around a single language, but they could not translate their skills for worldwide usage. Bob MacGregor explained, "On one of the early situations we ran into, we used the word *transparent*. Now in the United States, when you talk about a manager who is transparent, you are referring to somebody who advocates his position to others. So I can't give you an increase because the salary program doesn't allow me to do that. So I'm transparent. So I'm advocating my role and taking ownership. Some of our other countries had a very difficult time trying to translate transparency because it was always related to a visual point of view that you could see through it. So you could see through it or it was clear or you advocated." So you had three definitions for the same word. So IBM quickly realized that it was necessary to ensure that all of their contents are done in the right context. MacGregor added, "And so that created a bit of a problem for us and again there were no vendors who were skilled in understanding that first, and second, to be able to say, 'okay, we can deal with it.' So again, that drove us to do a lot of our work internally" (MacGregor, personal interview, 2004).

How Is E-Learning Implemented?

Marketing E-Learning

In addition to using e-learning for training its own employees, IBM also provides e-learning management tools, authoring tools for content creation, platforms for online training, custom development services and pre-packaged content to other companies (Khirallah and Kolbasuk 2000). According to Teresa Golden, vice president of marketing and strategy, IBM, with its expertise in services, hardware, software, and learning, offers a wide variety of learning solutions to external customers. IBM offers a complete learning solution tailored to an organization's specific needs. These needs can include designing and implementing an enterprise-wide learning strategy, creating learning initiatives to enhance productivity, or implementing the underlying infrastructure to support e-learning (Golden, personal interview, 2004). For example, IBM Lotus Development provides software solutions on self-paced and collaborative learning capabilities (Moore 2001). IBM Global Services provides e-learning solutions to others (Cirillo and Silverstein 2002). IBM also offers e-learning courses online to other companies to train employees on their skills, knowledge, and competency (Freivalds 2000).

Voluntary

E-learning courses, for the most part, are voluntary at IBM. It's an important way to get early acceptance. Hoff said, "In order to make that motivating, we don't make a lot of things mandatory. We are careful about this." According to Hoff, if one of the senior executives deems something mandatory, he has to send out the appropriate communication explaining why this is so important. He should explain that they are asked to go through those Web lectures that relate to their industry, and that this is important because it is helpful to the delivery of value to their customers. The message should be focused and relevant (Hoff, personal interview, 2004).

User-Friendly Support

Another marketing tool is to have a tutor available in the learning center. According to Lau, people like to interact with people, especially at the early part of the e-learning experience. Having a tutor available on site will improve the success of e-learning. Lau said "If we expect them to do it after work or at home, the success rate is a lot lower because the motivational level is lower. High tech and low touch would be a problem" (Lau, personal interview, 2004).

Word of Mouth

Word of mouth is a very significant means of marketing e-learning. Peer group influence is an important way to propagate the use of e-learning. When Basic Blue was first rolled out, the first managers going through it used very little of the e-learning part of the program. They used it sporadically. As a result, some students did the work and many did not. Some came prepared and some didn't. Some, rather than spreading the work over six months, crammed it all into a weekend or two before they came to the lab. Wattendorf said, "But as the word of mouth spread, once they went through the lab, almost without exception, at the end of the lab, at the end of the week-long experience they would say, 'I wish I had known how valuable that e-learning is and would have been to me and I would have done it much better.' And they go back and they send that message out to the rest of the people who are still working through that first phase." Years later, there is a much better response to e-learning on the part of new managers that are going through the program.

The other change to Basic Blue was to include a mastery test for certain material that is very important for managers to understand. The test includes concepts that are very important to IBM to make sure that a manager doesn't make any mistakes. Wattendorf commented, "And so we want to make sure that they do understand what the business conduct guidelines are and how we expect them to treat people" (Wattendorf, personal interview, 2004).

Lewis said, "The wisdom is understanding what we are trying to do. Would technology be better than something else? Does this information need to be convenient? Would Web be easier than face-to-face?" (Lewis, personal interview, 2004).

Supporting Learners

Development Plan

At IBM, the individual development plan grows out of the relationship between the manager and the employee. There is a development cycle during which each employee is asked to put in place an individual development plan, and in building that plan, the employee will have discussions with his or her manager about what priorities he or she should focus on in that particular year. The manager will then build a personal plan that enables the employee to grow in the needed skill areas (Arrington, personal interview, 2004). The development plan forms the basis for making evaluations that impact employees' pay. It's an expectation that some development is taking place. So, in addition to meeting business goals such as sales targets, employees have required areas of development as well, and these are measured.

Regarding motivation to learn among the professional workforce, IBM has a competitive culture where lower tier performers are dropped. MacGregor said, "If you don't stay current and pass your performance, that means you dropped to the bottom and that puts you at risk. So a lot of our employees recognize this, and they go out and they continue to keep their skills updated" (MacGregor, personal interview, 2004).

Administration

There is an administration team that is monitoring each participant's progress. If administrators don't see progress being made right away, they'll send participants a note. If they still don't see any movement, another reminder will be sent. After that, the students will get a phone call. The administrators stay on top of the situation pretty closely because their objectives are to get students through phase one of the programs (MacGregor, personal interview, 2004). According to Denise Murphy, Administrator for Basic Blue, there is tremendous support to participants to make sure they are making progress along the way. This effort begins with a launch letter inviting the manager to attend. But the process for administration is not initiated until enrollment. Murphy said, "So from the moment you enroll, your name is generated." Communication from the administrator at the beginning is more frequent, in the middle it's less frequent, and by the end it becomes very frequent. Participants could be frustrated for technical difficulties such as navigation or connectivity. They could have workload problems, or their problems could be content related. The administrator is always there to guide the participants along. About two months before the participants attend the lab, the reminder process kicks into high gear. For those that require a higher administrative touch, a process is in place that reaches them weekly, starting nine weeks prior to the beginning of lab class. Murphy said, "When I lose someone, it's a personal thing. Now, sometimes, losing people is out of my control. That involves emergency, medical, and family reasons. But if I lose somebody because it hasn't been explained to him or her properly or because work hasn't allowed him or her to complete the assignment, I feel as if I haven't done the best that I could to create that environment for the individual to train" (Murphy, personal interview, 2004).

When managers arrive for the face-to-face lab, some of them want to meet the administrators who helped them through the whole phase one process. MacGregor said, "And it's almost like, if you don't come, I'm taking that personally. So they develop the relationships. So that's what drives the success" (MacGregor, personal interview, 2004).

Help Desk

High tech/high touch can be done in a number of ways. The first option is to use an online instructor so employees can have easy access for help. Users just have to press a button and someone stationed 24/7 will help those who are online. Another way is have a phone number that they can call and ask for help.

A second approach is to have a tutor at the learning center. This will provide immediate help. For Basic Blue, a facilitator is available at the learning center every single day during the week. The participants are aware of who the facilitators are, so if they really have burning questions, they can meet or call the facilitator. From time to time, they may be struggling with one of the mastery tests, and they can call the facilitator. After the discussion, the facilitator then can give them credit for passing that module without having them go through the mastery test. MacGregor remarked, "So, it's little things like that where you say, 'hey, this is terrific. I had this dialogue and I don't have to go back and redo the thing I was having trouble with. The facilitator took care of that' " (MacGregor, personal interview, 2004).

The third approach is to help the learner with a buddy system where two people are paired up as a team to learn a module together. This allows a venue for frequent two-way communication.

And the fourth approach is to use management support and advice. Lau explained, "We found that one of the best practices is when the learner goes into an e-learning program and the manager tells him that he is just so excited about him taking e-learning because this is important to the learner's job." This is a pep talk to encourage the user to use e-learning. This is particularly important if it's a long module that is difficult to go through. If the module is a series of modules that takes a couple of weeks, then the manager will need to ask learners how they are doing from time to time. Lau said, "We find those managers or supervisors or mentors in the learning environment will have the high-touch for that individual and the learning really makes a difference compared to those without that kind of help. And if we have the manager supporting it, at the end, it will really accelerate the learning application on the job" (Lau, personal interview, 2004).

Language

IBM's management training is typically done in English. This is necessary in most of the face-to-face programs where there are people from different countries. So if they are in Asia and they have some managers from Singapore, China, India, and Malaysia together in the same room, English is used as the common language. This is also true for Europe. If there were a class in which there are Spanish-, Italian-, German-, French-, and English-speaking students in the same room, the common language again would be English (MacGregor, personal interview, 2004).

They would do the training in a different language if the facilitator and the participants were from a single country. MacGregor said, "I was talking to one of our facilitators who was doing a program in Israel and during the discussion that went on within the work group, it was all done in the country's language, but the report was done in English." That's common. If they are dealing with the sales team that is working with global accounts, they will do it in English because they are dealing with global accounts. However, if it happens to be a sales team that's in a small or medium business and it does all of its work in a single country, like Germany, then they will train in German (MacGregor, personal interview, 2004).

Time for E-Learning

Although management philosophy is to provide time for doing e-learning during work hours, in practice, this is often difficult for employees to do because of their heavy workloads and busy schedule. So they often end up doing e-learning on nights or weekends.

For Basic Blue, management's intent is to set time aside for e-learning, but the reality is that managers are more apt to do e-learning on their own time rather than taking two hours off to do e-learning during work. If they took off two hours during the day, they would end up working their regular job at night. The job simply doesn't go away. Wattendorf said, "If you ask me how many hours I'm going to take off to do learning, there aren't any. It's just this thing that gets added on" (Wattendorf, personal interview, 2004). Sanford added, "I went through Basic Blue training and that's exactly what I did. I pretty much did it in the evenings and on weekends. But the thing that motivated me to do it was that it was a prerequisite for the course, so I couldn't attend the class unless I'd taken and passed those exams" (Sanford, personal interview, 2004). Arrington continued, "It's not like we can take our jobs and set them aside. We readily accept and understand that this training may take us into late evenings or weekends. I think this is a culture that works, where work-life balance is something that they challenge. I think that most of us know it's not a nine-to-five job under normal circumstances and it's just something that we understand in today's environment" (Arrington, personal interview, 2004). These reactions were common when I spoke to other participants during my visits to IBM. Weintraub said, "What we find though is that people complain that they end up having to do it on off hours and there's going to be some of that no matter what, because it's impossible to really keep up unless you're doing learning outside of the normal hours" (Weintraub, personal interview, 2004). Furthermore, even when a Web-based training is required, it still doesn't mean someone lets up on his other priorities at work. The practical reality of life is that a lot of times people will find that this work is done after 10 P.M.

Confidentiality

The learning management system is an assessment tool in a sense. The various personal feedbacks are visible on the Web, but the details are not released to the manager or anybody else. Managers simply need to know that an individual passed a required course, rather than know the score or how many times the individual took the test. For voluntary courses for individuals' development purposes, scores are accessible only to the individual (Wattendorf, personal interview, 2004).

Supporting Instructors

Changing Role

E-learning requires a very different set of teaching skills than classroom teaching. In the classroom, the instructor is teaching a class with the view of the entire class. In the e-learning world, the instructor is facilitating discussion without seeing the audience. In this situation, the teacher has to be much more aggressive in eliciting interactions. The teacher may be a discussion facilitator rather than the subject matter expert. For example, if the instructor is dealing with a policy or operating issue, he or she would lead a discussion and have to be alert enough to spot the issue. MacGregor explained, "So if you say, 'I'm struggling with one of my employees who is having an absenteeism problem,' the initial dialogue may be what you are observing, but at some point in time the facilitator is going to pick up and ask if the person has a problem every Monday morning. Is it a drug or alcohol problem? The facilitator then would suggest talking to the HR and medical departments for further discussion. It's just very difficult to do that not having everyone in the same room" (MacGregor).

In Basic Blue, participants do their prework online. When they arrive, they discuss these issues in a classroom setting led by a facilitator. In terms of the facilitator's role, Jim Soltis, facilitator of Basic Blue, explained, "Well, what we're really doing is a lot of facilitated discussion on what they've learned online in the first phase about managerial style, organizational climate, coaching, and informational feedback. The importance of the learning lab is to really facilitate discussion around those issues" (Soltis, personal interview, 2004).

The facilitator has to be sensitive to the culture of the target audience. Some require a lot of solicitation to keep the group actively engaged, and others want to strictly adhere to preset schedules. MacGregor explained, "When you get into some of the Asian countries, they will agree with you on everything because they're very polite. So you have to ask the questions to see if they really understand what we're focused on. But in Germany they're very structured. They want to know what we are going to do at 9:15 in the morning and at 11:15. And if you say that we're going to end at 5, at 4:59 they're all packed up because you said we're going to end at 5, not at 5:05" (MacGregor, personal interview, 2004).

Training

Instructors do get training on facilitating e-learning classes. Most of IBM's training is done internally. Occasionally they will bring in external people to bring the facilitators' development to a higher level. John Wattendorf, Program Director Learning Design, said, "Because we have such a very strong emphasis on our leadership framework, we qualify our facilitators for use of that material." So after instructors go through their training, they are then observed to see how they use what they have learned as a facilitator. They're observed by a master trainer. They get feedback and they become qualified (Wattendorf, personal interview, 2004).

Corporate Support

IBM invests $1 billion on learning each year in developing their employees. A very large library of programs is available to employees on a 24/7 basis, and most of the courses are voluntary. MacGregor said, "Learning is extremely important" (MacGregor, personal interview, 2004). Managers are encouraged to promote e-learning (Weintraub, personal interview, 2004). Ted Hoff, chief learning officer, remarked, "We are tremendously blessed at IBM to have a century-long line of executives who care about learning. Fundamentally, Tom Watson Senior and Junior instilled in this company the fundamental belief that the company is much stronger if the company focuses on learning and its people. The phrase I use is that it is in the DNA of the company. I really do believe that" (Hoff, personal interview, 2004).

Learning Management System

IBM Lotus learning management system (LMS) handles instructor-led and online training for its global community and covers more than 30 languages. It's a platform is used to train its employees, customers, suppliers, and business partners (Donovan 2003). The LMS, with its e-learning components, is designed to connect to other applications and learning products (Moore 2003). It is designed to manipulate all shared content object reference model (SCORM) compliant content. SCORM, which is a set of e-learning specifications compiled by the U.S. government's Advanced Distributed Learning initiative to support interoperability.

IBM also has a sophisticated learning-content management system (LCMS), which provides performance support, a blended program for leadership training, and an online e-coach to guide managers in creating personal development plans. On management development, software called Edvisor offers users three tracks to manage their training. The first track includes hundreds of online best practices management support modules called Quickviews. These were co-developed with Harvard Business School Publishing and represent the best critical thinking on management development. On-line Quickview is a fast way to get an overview and to access basic information on a particular subject. It contains stories, traps, and other helpful tools. Learners can review scenarios multiple times. MacGregor said, "So I can go through this once and then I can come back and do it again and again. There are actually 5,000 screens in our coaching scenarios" (MacGregor, personal interview, 2004). The second track assesses the learners' activities prior to the face-to-face lab session. This allows learners to be prepared and make the best use of their time when they get together. For Basic Blue, the administrators monitor students' e-learning progress for the first six months. Surveys are conducted after the six-month period as well, and feedback is received at that time (MacGregor, personal interview, 2004). The third track is the intelligent agent, which tracks the participants' 360 degree leadership survey feedback. The 360 evaluations and the Herman Brain Dominance surveys (HBDI) results are used to determine gaps in management skills. Edvisor then offers advice in building a personalized development plan (Schettler 2002).

For IBM's employees, the LMS is the portal to access course catalogs, register for courses, assess and enhance their skills.

Collaborative Spaces

IBM has 25,000 collaborative spaces that allow teams of people who have common interests or work in common areas to have discussions on the Internet. This allows these teams to work together. They are able to share information across the team. For example, in sales and distribution collaborative space, there is something called "sellers connection," which is an online system where learners can get help from experts. If a learner has a particular sales situation that he or she has not encountered before, the learner could put a question into the system and those people who are registered in the system as experts will respond to the question. These experts can be anywhere in the world. What they would then do is to explain how they would handle that situation or a similar challenge (McLaughlin, personal interview, 2004). For a management-development collaborative space, someone may have a question about employee absenteeism. MacGregor explained the dynamics of discussion in this space, "So I've got an employee who's not coming to work on time. I've tried everything, but I don't know what to do next. So you would put that in your space. Then you get others responding. They'd say 'I had something like that at work and this is what I did at work.' Somebody else comes in and says, 'I tried the same thing and it didn't work.' So you have that whole discussion of what's going on." This is a way for the person to learn about the complexity of the situation and also learn from others who have gone through a similar experience (MacGregor, personal interview, 2004).

How Is Effectiveness Determined by Corporations?

Methods of Measurement

When it comes to effectiveness of e-learning, IBM measures every level of the process. Lewis said, "I use that city metaphor, New York City, buildings, people, furniture." Evaluation needs to happen at each level distinctly. If the city is your business, you have to generate business and revenue. You have to ask yourself, what's ROI? IBM typically uses the four levels of the Kirkpatrick model. Lewis added, "We get down to furniture level. So we take a lot of care to take time out to study things at every level, city ROI to furniture" (Lewis, personal interview, 2004). Hoff also said that IBM does an enormous amount of measurement and that it's a massive challenge in the whole field of learning. Hoff said, "Let me tell you what we have been doing and what we will be doing in the future. We do use the Kirkpatrick model of measurement but we also use a different approach." The different approach goes beyond the Kirkpatrick model and measuring external customer satisfaction.

IBM's goal is to develop a common standard for measuring effectiveness of e-learning to achieve uniformity among the various businesses under IBM. Chak Lau, evaluation expert, explained, "IBM can use the same methodology, the same set of tools, the same set of surveys, same set of interview protocols, same way to analyze and the same way to report it. The most important part is we want standardization across IBM" (Lau, personal interview, 2004).

The Kirkpatrick model has four basic levels. Level 1 is participants' reaction to the learning. It's asking participants what they think of the program. Level 2 refers to what learning is gained. That is, how much additional knowledge was gained by training and whether participants have learned to do something differently. Level 3 is applying the learning. Are people reporting that they have taken action based upon learning? Are they getting better by using e-learning techniques? Are people posting their actions to share with others? This then is a way to track whether people have taken action. Level 4 is the impact of learning on business. It measures whether it adds up to improvement in business. Sometime people split level 4 into level 4 and 5. Level 5 is the measure of ROI. Level 4 actually implies level 5.

Kirkpatrick Level 1

Level 1 is a survey of users' reactions to a course. That is, did they like the course or not. For Basic Blue, based on 11,000 respondents, the feedback was 1.02 on a scale of 1 to 5, 1 being the top rating. MacGregor said, "You can't get much better than that." Other ratings include the ability to do required lessons at 1.29, the learning lab experience at 1.14, and recommendation to others at 99.9 percent. MacGregor said, "So these are the kinds of measurements that I get year after year. So my objective is to maintain these kinds of measurements and make sure that we're hitting the mark on everything that we do" (MacGregor, personal interview, 2004).

IBM gets feedback from participants on the courses and the facilitators. That feedback comes back to the development team in the form of suggestions and requests in those areas that are outdated or need change (Wattendorf, personal interview, 2004). The feedback is a continual process. Based on the feedback over the first two years, there were more than 300 changes made to the Basic Blue program in terms of both technology and content. Based on survey results, a progress bar was added to the learning space so that participants could see how they are doing relative to their efforts. Regarding feedback on content, MacGregor explained, "What we heard back was, 'don't just give me a talking head.' If you got somebody that you're going to use video or some audio on, it ought to be somebody that I can directly relate to and somebody that I should be listening to. So it might be the CEO, it might be one of the senior executives, but don't put a middle-level executive in there. Then it's important for me to hear directly from them" (MacGregor, personal interview, 2004).

IBM tracks the usage rates either through something as formal as a focus group or something as informal as just getting feedback from people. Hoff said, "So when you look at Basic Blue, they do step aside on a regular basis at those events, to ask the new managers what has been most valuable to them here and what do they think we should do next to improve. We ask in a fairly open way and then we asked it in some specific ways. But in my opinion, there is nothing like asking the participants directly as your principal source of insight about whether something is valuable or not" (Hoff, personal interview, 2004).

IBM has a set of leadership competencies, which were designed for their executives. So a skills assessment allows them to focus on those things that separate good managers from extraordinary managers. MacGregor said, "So we have behaviors under each of the competencies and through our 360 instrument, we measure how well the manager is able to demonstrate those behaviors to their subordinates, peers, or manager" (MacGregor, personal interview, 2004).

Participants continue to provide feedback on Basic Blue because their comments and recommendations are routinely followed up. A Harvard professor was hired to do 10 to 15 minute interviews to solicit feedback from participants. According to MacGregor, her average interview lasted for over an hour and a half instead. When she asked the participants why they spent so much time with her, they told her that they do so because their response was followed up every time (MacGregor, personal interview, 2004).

Matt McLaughlin, a learning leader, said, "You cannot become complacent and assume that if you're doing something well today, it's going to be well accepted in the future. You have to keep working ahead to the new requirements, especially from a business perspective, and you need to be very well aware of the technology and the methodologies that outside companies and vendors have." According to McLaughlin, learners have to be engaged on an ongoing basis in a variety of forms to make sure that their requirements are met and that the learning is delivering value (McLaughlin, personal interview, 2004).

Kirkpatrick Level 2

There are some requisite skills or knowledge that need to be mastered in each course. For example, there are certain contents within Basic Blue that students are expected to master. This could include performance management, compensation, or other required skills. A mastery test covers those subjects. If users pass the mastery test, then they are ready to build upon that basic knowledge in the face-to-face module (MacGregor, personal interview, 2004).

The online mastery test just requires the participants to get through it. So if the student answers a question incorrectly, he or she can go back and try it again. It will tell the student where to go to look up the answer. The student is not expected to memorize the material. The key is that at least at one point in time, the student knew what the correct answer was (Wattendorf, personal interview, 2004).

MacGregor said, "We know that we had improvement because of our mastery test. So that gave us a pretty good feel that we were on the right track. I have lunch with the managers who are here almost every day when we're running classes. So I talk to about 1,000 managers a year" (MacGregor, personal interview, 2004).

Kirkpatrick Level 3

Level 3 measures the application of what's learned in the class. That is, how is the learning transferring to the job, and is there change in behavior. The 360 survey is done prior to Basic Blue to identify skill gaps and then the survey is taken again at a later time to see if the gaps have narrowed and to see if the users are on the right track. MacGregor said, "Now we do realize there are some environmental issues that will impact the survey. But over a period of time, if, in fact, we're seeing things improve, then we're on the right track" (MacGregor, personal interview, 2004).

For Basic Blue, a survey is done six months after the completion of the program to see if there are some differences in performance. A chain of impact analysis is done where the following questions are asked: What were the focus areas or the objectives of Basic Blue? What things are you doing differently? What did you observe? What impact did those things have on your subordinates? Did that have a positive or negative impact on your department and how? How did that impact specific business results? MacGregor explained, "We realize it's self-reporting, so that's a negative, but we think if a manager can describe all of those stages, we've got a pretty good connection. If they can describe all that and can describe how they came up with a monetary figure for that, it's not too bad" (MacGregor, personal interview, 2004).

Kirkpatrick Level 4

Level 4 deals with calculation of savings associated with e-learning. The savings result from a number of factors. First, the e-learning module is shorter in time in covering the same content in comparison to a classroom situation. E-learning, unlike classroom learning, does not have socialization and gathering time required for running a classroom. Second, savings result from avoided travel costs and associated expenses. Third, potential productivity savings could be achieved if e-learning results in a more efficient way of doing work or a different way of doing business. According to Lau, productivity is more difficult to measure because it's difficult to isolate the impact of a single factor in a work environment that is influenced by multiple factors. E-learning just takes less time than classroom to present content. According to Lau, a one-hour module of material on e-learning is equivalent to about two hours of traditional classroom learning. A four-hour module is equivalent to one day of instruction. Compression of time translates to savings. There are also savings associated with lodging, rental cars, meals, incidental costs, development costs, delivery costs, classroom and instructor costs.

However, the development cost of e-learning is a lot more expensive than the development of a traditional classroom instructor-led course. According to Lau, sometimes it's five times to even ten times the cost but the increased development cost is just a one-time expense. In a traditional class, every time new people come in, more cost is being incurred. Lau said, "So that's why you can come up with a cost model for e-learning versus traditional training. You have a lot of savings" (Lau, personal interview, 2004).

MacGregor said, "If I were to deliver it all face-to-face for our Basic Blue program it would cost me a little over $13,000. I can do it for less than $9,000 using blended learning." That's more than 30 percent in savings. That's very substantial considering the program covers over 30,000 managers. MacGregor explained, "What I did was to spread the development cost over a three-year period. It's a comprehensive approach to try to get a cost comparison. It tells me that this is a cost effective way of delivery" (MacGregor, personal interview, 2004).

IBM corporate provides unlimited universal access to e-learning for all employees globally. According to Zinsi, in 2003, e-learning student days totaled 788,557. In the first half of 2004, e-learning days totaled 519,322. One e-learning day equals six hours. In 2003, 48 percent of all learning was delivered via e-learning. In the first half of 2004, 54 percent of all learning was delivered via e-learning. The approximate cost avoidance is $367 for an e-learning day (Zinzi, personal interview, 2004).

Beyond Kirkpatrick—IBM's ACE Model

IBM's latest innovation is an effectiveness model that goes beyond the traditional Kirkpatrick model. According to Lau, the Kirkpatrick model is more focused on the learning event itself and its effectiveness. That effectiveness measurement includes increased knowledge, application of knowledge, and impact of knowledge on the business. However, the learning might affect the customer interface as well. The additional impact is whether the customer is satisfied with the service. Lau said, "So we should go beyond just the learning event itself, so that's why I think the Kirkpatrick model is necessary, but not sufficient. Kirkpatrick model is just internally reduced cost avoidance or cost savings" (Lau, personal interview, 2004). But what does customer satisfaction mean? Lau explained, "For example, if you have a team of electricians working on a building project and they have learned the skills to do it, they are so fulfilled because they know how to do the new circuit design. When they face the customer, they also know how to explain the design, and the customer is satisfied with that kind of explanation and the new way of doing things. So the employees are satisfied to learn and will project that kind of satisfaction to the customer, and the customer in turn will say, I'm satisfied with the service you are providing to me" (Lau, personal interview, 2004).

IBM's ACE Model

ACE is a new accountability model. It stands for accountability, context, and effectiveness (ACE). It's at the beginning stage of application at IBM. The accountability model calls for the learner to be accountable for his learning. That means the learners should be motivated and diligent in learning all the materials. The supervisor should manage and support the learners so that when they do the work they are coached to succeed. There are four partners in the accountability of a learning program. First, it's the learner himself. Second, it's the designer of the learning program. Third, it's the deliverer, which is the instructor or facilitator. Fourth, it is the manager who needs to support the learning program. In the middle, there is also a need for support in the context of an organization. The organization provides the resources to enable learners to acquire skills and knowledge. Resources include such things as the right tools, the right environment and the right process (Lau, personal interview, 2004).

Soft Measures

According to Lau, based on research studies, learning is not only just conveying skills and knowledge to employees. Learning can be a factor in retaining employees because they feel that the company really cares about them. Employees' morale is also related to learning. Lau explained, "We never can prove how much learning contributes to employee morale. But some of those companies that don't have comprehensive learning programs tend to have high attrition rates" (Lau, personal interview, 2004).

What Lessons Are Learned?

Failure at the Learner Level

The first lessons are to understand the nature of the target audience and recognize the level of human touch required in a learning program. IBM had some lessons learned in this area. For example, IBM was hiring a lot of people in Asia, so they were assuming that because India is high-tech, that e-learning might take place faster in India. They assumed that because these people learned English and are technically literate, they would gravitate to e-learning much more easily than Americans. That was not the case because these people needed to talk to human beings at some point. Hoff explained, "It's a lot like Maslow's hierarchy of need. E-learning will be very effective once you take care of people's basic needs. Otherwise they will not see the positive attributes of e-learning."

Managers also need to realize that e-learning is an efficient tool for their employees to learn. Wattendorf explained, "IBMers, probably like workers in most places, would still probably like to take two or three days off from work, attend a workshop, learn what they think they have to learn, and they've done their thing. They are less inclined to do the e-learning pre-work and attend a session that is more focused on work, almost like a business meeting and then take that out and apply it after it. So there really is a culture shift taking place in our efforts to help managers realize that they can be more efficient in their learning if we do it this way" (Wattendorf, personal interview, 2004).

Failure at the Product Level

Proper user engagement must be created. The ability of users to connect easily to the e-learning program is an important consideration. Poor user engagement could be a disaster. According to Lewis, IBM encountered a big problem with user engagement when Basic Blue was first rolled out. Lewis said that the writing was brilliant. The curriculum design and development for the content and the learning systems to support the environment took a substantial amount of effort. However, this effort was dwarfed by all the instruction and care that had to be done in creating the workable user engagement. Lewis explained, "Plug-in use is only one example. There were people who didn't even know what IBM's enterprise is. They actually had to make 800 changes on user engagement, including creating a button so that anyone could do it" (Lewis, personal interview, 2004).

Another lesson learned is to state the objectives upfront and make sure that the requirements are clearly stated. Sanford said, "I would think one of the lessons learned that I have experienced is probably just making sure that we actually take the time and go through the requirement process to ensure that we fully understand what the requirements are before we develop a solution." Arrington, learning leader at IBM Corporate, added, "The better the planning is up front, the better the solution" (Arrington, personal interview, 2004). Sanford said, "We did an assessment several years ago and we talked about all this money IBM's been investing in learning and took a look at what the learning investment was. What we discovered was that the majority of the learning investment was being spent on strategic objectives and priorities, and it wasn't really being spent on increasing the skills that would increase employees skills in order to deliver the business objective" (Sanford, personal interview, 2004).

Content must be of high quality also. According to Weintraub, bad content could be a problem in the e-learning space because there is no instructor there that could shift the focus of the class. Weintraub said, "I guess that's another lesson that I learned. Bad training is bad training, and if something is designed well with the audience in mind, we get very few complaints. The benefit of being in a classroom is that you can make more mistakes in the design, because the instructor can change on the fly very easily, and it's harder to do so in an e-learning situation." It's important that e-learning is more structured in design. The right design principles or right adult learning principles have to be followed. The requirements have to be established in a rigorous manner so that the audience is getting something they really need to know (Weintraub, personal interview, 2004).

Content must be relevant. IBM in the mid- to late-1990s flooded their employees with e-learning courses. The idea of having massive numbers of courses on a Web site that people could tap into backfired. IBM quickly realized that that is not effective learning. E-learning has to be focused and made relevant to the work environment (Hoff, personal interview, 2004).

Mastery tests must be designed properly. Lewis explained, "I remember when we implemented the Basic Blue program. Over 60 percent of the managers were failing the sexual-harassment test. The test we wrote was horrible. But evaluating things dynamically is important and it allows you to improve continuously" (Lewis, personal interview, 2004).

Finally, e-learning can also be added to complement face-to-face programs and thus improve learner satisfaction. IBM has a program for new employees called YOURIBM. This is a revision of the old program called Becoming One Voice. In developing the new program, IBM concluded that the problem with old program was that it was solely face-to-face for two days for a new employee. Hoff said, "There is a limit to what you can do in two days face-to-face, and we weren't getting enough out to the new employees. Now it's one-year experience but still two and a half days face-to-face, but a lot of prework is done over the Internet during the year. New YOURIBM satisfaction rate is much higher. It went from 59 percent to 79 percent" (Hoff, personal interview, 2004).

Failure at the Organizational Level

Underestimating the challenges faced by e-learning instructors is also a problem. The facilitator in e-learning plays a role very different from a classroom instructor. As a former teacher himself, Weintraub said, "I've been involved in learning for quite some time, even in the days before a lot was done over the Internet, when we were mostly using satellite, video, and so forth. One of the mistakes that people made was that they thought they could take anybody who's a good teacher and put them into an e-learning situation—a distance learning situation—and they would do fine. And that was absolutely not true. It's almost analogous to saying that an actor from the silent movies was going to be fine in the talkies." Unless these instructors understand how to use the technology well, how to keep people participating and active and how to use media in the ways that it needs to be used, including being interactive, stimulating, and using different techniques, then they're not going to be successful (Weintraub, personal interview, 2004).

Time has to be set aside for e-learning. A number of interviewees had indicated that although there is good intention to set aside time at the workplace to do e-learning, the practical reality is that most do the work during off-hours. Weintraub said, "The biggest thing is to really give people the time to do it and to recognize that, when they're learning something, that's part of their job, too" (Weintraub, personal interview, 2004)

Hoff explained that, right now, when they have anything face-to-face, students are given the dedicated time, but when it's pure e-learning, that often does not happen. If users are constantly thwarted in attempting to use e-learning, they will be discouraged. If the manager repeatedly interrupts e-learning, users will not try it anymore. Hoff said, "The next thing you know, you've been told three times, the manager says I believe in it, but not right now. You don't ask the fourth time" (Hoff, personal interview, 2004).

5

ANALYSIS

This chapter is an analysis of how IBM's e-learning experiences compare with other corporations. IBM and other corporations have aspects of e-learning that they excel in as well as areas that may require further enhancements. Their experiences and lessons learned should serve as an important guide to those who are implementing e-learning.

Significant Events

IBM had a significant corporate event that accelerated the development of e-learning. For IBM, it was the appointment of the chief learning officer, to centralize learning at IBM, by former CEO Lou Gerstner that catapulted the wide use of e-learning. At that time, training had been fragmented and the sheer size of the company clearly called for the need of a chief learning officer to oversee activities of the entire learning community at IBM. E-learning was an important means to provide the ability to facilitate learning in a global community. The important context is that IBM is a huge global company with more than 300,000 people doing business in 178 countries. Because 40 percent of their employees are mobile at any point in time, they had to leverage technology to address that issue.

Another corporation I examined had a significant event when the former CEO called for a comprehensive internal audit, which led to the discovery of many redundant training programs and the opportunity to use e-learning on a large scale. The audit investigated such areas as the kind of training that was done, when it was done, who it was done by, and what the cost was. According to the chief learning officer, the process started with an examination of the course catalog across the company to consolidate redundancies, eliminate gaps, and untangle overlaps. As one example, they found 48 separate common courses on effective presentation, ranging from two to eight hours. By analyzing the data, they were able to identify functional areas such as finance, IT, sales, professional skills, human resources, and environmental health and safety (EH and S) that have certain commonalities across multiple businesses. They found that less than 30 percent of course material was determined to be truly distinct. More than 1,600 courses were eliminated in the first year. Without rationalization of courses and centralizing common curriculum, they would have had a tremendous amount of redundancies and would have been paying much more to digitize content.

Another corporation I examined had merger activities that provided a special impetus to streamline and combine their resources toward a common goal in e-learning.

Organization

A key component of implementing e-learning is to have the right learning structure. IBM has an excellent centralized learning structure under the leadership of a chief learning officer (CLO) who oversees the entire learning community at IBM. The CLO has eight account executives who are the clients that serve as the interface with line organizations. They are integrated with line organizations, understand their business objectives, and develop business solutions for them. Together, they meet with the CLO on a regular basis to share ideas, set priorities, and maintain corporate standards. These account executives know the business objectives of line organizations they represent as well as the overall vision of the company. They act as advocates for the line organizations, but at the same time they see their role as a part of the entire IBM learning community.

Another corporation I examined has a centralized learning structure in form but it operates in a totally decentralized fashion in practice. It is a conglomerate with different and distinct businesses—each is a profit center and operates very independently from one another. Each is autonomous in operation and in its learning structure. Thus, the CLO has minimal oversight of their operations. The learning structure is a dotted line relationship between learning leaders from line organizations and the

Chief Learning Officer. These learning leaders do not report directly to the CLO. They have full autonomy to do what they wish to do. They are free to inform the CLO, but they don't have the obligation to do so. Thus, each business has its own way of carrying out training. Consequently, each organization approaches e-learning in its own way. With the exception of some minimal guideline on common platform and protocol, each business carries out its own learning programs. Under these circumstances, the learning structure can appear to be fragmented, with a different learning solution going from one business unit to the next, but it's a formula that works for them. Unlike a single product or service company, they have multiple products and services in multiple businesses that are very diverse. One size just doesn't fit all. Of course, for those learning areas such as ethics and safety, which cut across multiple organizations, the corporate learning organization will assume sponsorship under the leadership of the CLO. The CLO's primary focus is on leadership training for upper management. He considers high-level leadership training as complex and, therefore, would call for face-to-face sessions. He believes that there is no substitute for high-level learning, where experts learn from each other. They offer executive leadership training courses for different levels of executives. These courses require e-learning for prework followed by face-to-face learning at a corporate training center.

Another corporation I examined is largely an operating company that has a large number of weekly workers and a much smaller proportion of professional employees. It also has a centralized learning organization with account executives assigned to business units. Their goal is to do it faster and cheaper and train as many people as they can, within the shortest amount of time, and at the lowest costs. Their e-learning programs have a greater focus on skills training and first- and second-line supervisory training. Their learning programs are far more operations oriented. Their leadership training of upper management is primarily outsourced. They place a greater emphasis on technology, which they believe is the gateway to content. They believe that if learners can't get access, the quality of content will not matter much. They have workers who need to get training in skill areas such as splicing and installation of telecommunications services. These training courses are needed for them to perform their jobs in the field, so they set aside time for employees to learn. However, for the weekly employees, having to do learning during off hours is less of an issue, because time is provided during working hours for such purposes. They strive to standardize their training so that employees are interchangeable and can shift from location to location and be able to immediately perform because the training is the same. The employees often have to respond to storms and emergencies in other regions, and interchangeability is useful. Blue-collar training, technician training, pole climbing, and splicing are still done 100 percent in house.

Why E-Learning?

IBM uses e-learning because it is faster and cheaper than classroom training and because it reaches a global audience. IBM's strategic reason is that they have a division that markets e-learning hardware and software. Their business is technology, so they have a natural inclination to drive to the cutting edge of technology. IBM constantly looks to find innovative ways to use e-learning. Their most recent on-demand e-learning strategy is an excellent illustration. On demand shifts the focus of learning in classrooms to the learner at the workplace on a real- time basis. This is a dramatic departure from our traditional approach of learning the content first and subsequently applying it in the workplace. This latest strategy is simple, but the implication can be quite significant. The underlying principle is that learning is brought immediately to the workplace. On-demand learning addresses the challenges that a person faces everyday and provides a tool to solve that particular problem. When e-learning is being applied, it must be relevant and focused for the target audience. The CLO explained that the idea of indiscriminately having massive numbers of courses up on a Web site that people could tap into doesn't work. People say that that is not effective learning. Effective e-learning comes from experience.

Another corporation I examined has a strategic reason to expand in its global market. It has a reputation for being a premier multiple-product corporation with a substantial global presence. Therefore, training is geared to a diverse group of employees in their global learning community. The bottom line goal is to achieve savings for the business. A senior learning leader said that the company definitely is aligned with what it needs to do to support business goals. If the company can't prove that it is providing value, it won't use the training tool. At the business level, a business case has to be made and must tie into the CEO's strategic goals. The key is to ask if e-learning makes sense from a financial perspective. In order to get funding, a business case has to be demonstrated. Relevant questions include: How much money is currently being spent on training? How many people need to get training? How can e-learning be delivered? Generally, if the training doesn't require some hands-on type of activity, it can be delivered effectively through asynchronized sessions. A senior learning leader said that first managers make the business case. Are they going to save any money by doing e-learning? Then, secondly, can they use e-learning effectively? According to the chief information officer, classroom training is not always practical and cost effective. He said that what they found is two things. One is that they could never get enough people through training centers to satisfy all the learning needs, so, face-to-face learning wasn't always the option. The other thing they found is that it's not always economical to do classroom training. Some people don't necessarily want to take that time away from the office for classroom learning. It's expensive to fly people into a corporate center and pay board for them for a week or a few weeks. Therefore, learning is often delivered in a multimedia environment with some face-to-face, some classroom, and some self-paced e-learning. A right blend of modules should be selected, whether it's for leadership or technical courses. Another reason for implementing e-learning is the benefit of completing preclass work prior to in-class sessions so that everyone starts from a common point. It's simply more efficient to conduct the class when participants come with the same degree of preparation. E-learning for prework is an excellent way to establish a threshold knowledge requirement for the class. Another reason for using e-learning is to standardize curriculum. The key value of digitization is to bring training to a common standard and eliminate variations. They have an excellent approach to reach their learning community across regions and languages by using a layered approach in designing e-learning courses. The first layer contains content that is common to everyone. The next layer would superimpose national and regional differences, and the third layer could be departmental differences. In this layered fashion, they can best use the e-learning course material in the most efficient way. To be a successful global company, speed to market is very important and standardization facilitates that process. Thus, standardization is significant for this corporation, as is the ability to train people in different countries with different languages in a quick, cost effective, and consistent manner.

Another corporation I examined is primarily concerned with providing reliable telecommunications services to their customers. Their motivation to standardize training is to enable their field workers to have the flexibility of responding to weather-related emergencies anywhere in the country. Their corporate strategy focuses on efficiencies and revenue growth, and training is an integral part of revenue growth. When asked what he expected to accomplish through e-learning, the chief e-learning architect said that, first, they expect to reduce the cost of training. Second, they want training to be available to all employees anywhere and anytime, at work, home, Internet café, and so forth. Third, they want to make training available to their employees at critical, time-sensitive windows of opportunity for new product launches, and for critical corporate policy compliance. Fourth, they'd like to think of their training, which offers over 1,500 e-learning courses at no cost to departments or employees, as a loyalty and retention benefit. The bulk of their e-learning application is just-in-time training. They focus on improving their internal processes to get faster, better, and cheaper. A few years ago, they were faced with a challenging situation to train thousands of employees quickly. They were saddled with the anticipation of simultaneous retirement of 40,000 skilled personnel. That meant they had to train 40,000 employees with limited resources and within a limited window of time. As such, they had to reengineer their approach to training, and e-learning became a vital part of its reengineered training.

Historically, training was done differently across the country. It depended somewhat on an individual instructor's knowledge and preference. There was little or no control over what an instructor in a classroom in Southern California was teaching or what an instructor in New York City was teaching. Those two instructors could have been teaching the same thing but very differently or they may have been teaching entirely different things. This difference created a problem when people moved from one location to another location. They may not have been following the same processes of doing things the same way. They may not even have been using the same tools. Standardization through e-learning was a feasible way to provide consistency in training. The importance of employees getting the same training was explained by the chief learning officer: For example, Florida is the lightning capital of America, and bonding and grounding their work is the most critical thing that they could possibly ever do. Without a proper ground, that particular section of telecommunication wire will require service in a very short time, and so will everybody's phones, so if that's not done properly, in a standard consistent way, it meant some teachers weren't teaching it. What if they need to move workforce from Florida to Newark, because there's a disaster, or New York to Florida or New York to California? If there are legitimate differences in a particular situation, they have different versions of the course for different people in geographic locations. If someone in Virginia does things a little bit differently or has to do things a little differently, there's the same course, with just a section of it a little bit different.

How Is E-Learning Developed?

Business Objectives

IBM defines business objectives as the starting point in developing learning requirements. It uses a collaborative process that involves the content experts, designers, developers, and technology and infrastructure specialists. They gather input from learners and instructors as well. Once the learning content is selected to meet business objectives, the next step is to determine what portion of the content should be delivered via e-learning. The process should be carried out systematically so that e-learning is used only when it's the most appropriate vehicle to deliver that content or a portion of that content. IBM is a technology company so it has a natural bias to push technology and use e-learning. Yet it is very disciplined in its approach by using a four-tier model as a logical way to determine what content should be delivered through e-learning. Tier one refers to learning from plain information. E-learning tools such as Web lectures, Web books, Web conferences, Web pages and videos would be applicable. Tier two calls for learning from interaction. E-learning techniques such as interactive games, coaching, simulation, and self-directed learning objects would be applicable. Tier three is learning from collaboration. E-learning is still applicable by using live virtual classes, e-labs, collaborative sessions, and live conferences. The first two levels are done through self-paced e-learning. The third is done through synchronous e-learning where it's given at a specified time, but learners can be in the same or different locations. Tier four calls for learning from collocation, which is reserved for face-to-face sessions. It includes classroom sessions, learning labs, mentoring, role playing, expert presentation, and motivation speeches (IBM 2004).

Another corporation I examined said that it is important to state clearly from the beginning what the students are expected to get from the course. Without the stated objective, it is difficult to measure the outcome of a course, so the first task is to be clear about the objectives. The second task is to avoid technical difficulties. Learners will just not come back if there is not enough bandwidth or if their PCs are not compatible with the software. The corporation uses a model that looks at the complexity of the content to determine whether e-learning should be used to deliver that particular content. For simple concepts and cognitive learning, it will use e-learning. For highly complex, interactive, and specialized training, it will use classroom learning. It will also use classroom learning if the corporation wants to use peer group pressure to influence a behavior change.

Project Management

E-learning has numerous discrete components such as content, design, and delivery systems that are both independent and interdependent. Each component has to be done well in its own right, but each also has to be integrated with other components to effectively deliver the ultimate e-learning product to the learners. IBM has specialists dedicated in each of the many areas of e-learning, such as content experts, designers, developers, technologists, and even an expert in performance measurements. These e-learning professionals are experts in their areas, but they also have a very good grasp of how their own tasks fit into the overall e-learning development process. IBM's selection of experienced line managers as e-learning instructors is an excellent way to facilitate practical learning experience needed in the workplace. IBM provides a common platform for sharing information and a common standard for measuring effectiveness.

Another corporation I examined has a team of experts and professionals work together to develop e-learning. A senior learning leader gave an example with subject matter experts, instructional designers, and graphic developers who make up the core team that builds e-learning. The graphic developers will take a curriculum outline and work on it from the graphics perspective and put details on interactive features. The designers will put together a graphic storyboard which will show what the course will look like. This is a collaborative effort and a great deal of dialogue flows back and forth among subject-matter experts.

Another corporation I examined has the account executive (AE) as the person representing a business unit's interest. He seeks input from subject-matter experts and relies on a number of other project-management personnel to be involved in the e-learning decision. Ultimately, the AE is the project manger responsible for delivering the e-learning initiative. If the AE reviews the content and decides that it has application in more than one business unit, more often than not, the AE will seek corporate funding for e-learning because the content and the investment can be spread over a larger audience. If, on other hand, the content is very unique or very specialized, then the business unit will fund it. There will be countless meetings and conference calls and usability tests will be conducted. In some cases, new server capacity will be required or existing applications will have to be adapted or recoded to support this new requirement. Therefore, from an e-learning architectural perspective, e-learning technology specialists will be involved in the process from beginning to end.

E-Learning versus Classroom Learning

IBM's CLO said that blended learning is taking the best features of classroom learning and e-learning and combining them into a blended approach. However, it is not always clear how best to balance the two components. Not every application is suitable for e-learning but the CLO wants to have a bias toward using e-learning to ensure that if something has to be done face-to-face, they will absolutely do it.

IBM's application of e-learning ranges from high technical skills training to leadership training. Typically, e-learning is used to deliver technical skills training courses. IBM goes further and uses e-learning to deliver leadership training courses as well. For example, their premier leadership program, called Basic Blue, for their high potential managers, is a masterful blend of e-learning and classroom instructions. The cognitive knowledge, mastery of information, and interactive simulations are all done by e-learning before the in-class face-to-face session. The feedback from the participants is most favorable. They have done all their preclass work, so when they arrive in class, they are using the class time optimally for interactivity among participants. The biggest learning experience is learning from one another, and that experience cannot be delivered by e-learning alone because one simply cannot anticipate all possible scenarios beforehand. Face-to-face interaction often triggers unanticipated scenarios that require unique solutions that occur spontaneously.

Another corporation I examined has a CLO who said that, in a teaching and learning environment, if something is simple, e-learning is best. It is simple and clear. Without a lot of complexity, e-learning is efficient and cost effective. However, when people go to the higher level courses, which are much more complex, learning has less to do with content and more to do with the context. As such, classroom training then becomes more suitable. This CLO explained that what you're doing then is helping students with nuances of both diagnosis and data intake and then the nuances of combination of what they know and what they're able to do for unique solutions. Actually, in many cases, classroom learning is combined with e-learning in a blended approach, and then e-learning is done prior to classroom. Classrooms can impart more than just basic knowledge. For example, teaching someone the rules of the road in driving is strictly cognitive and should be done online. However, classroom interaction will be required if students are asked to change their behavior toward drinking and driving. Group exercises and peer pressure are generally the type of things you put into a classroom curriculum if you're trying to change someone's behavior, because peer pressure will come into play.

Another CLO at corporation I examined said that e-learning and classroom learning are alternate means for learning. Each has positive and negative features. For example, one advantage of e-learning is that the learner can take the class repeatedly until the subject matter is mastered. Classroom learning, on the other hand, is more conducive to interactions and collaborations. Blended learning is a way to capture the best features of e-learning and classroom learning. According to the chief e-learning architect, e-learning is faster, cheaper, and sometimes better, but there's no amount of e-learning that can ever make up for a face-to-face session with a gifted instructor. He said that there is no substitute for a skilled teacher. He added that a piece of software will not inspire one to reach for the stars, but a good teacher will. E-learning simply can't replicate the classroom environment in its entirety. First, it is very difficult if not impossible, to anticipate every single possibility, every single scenario. Second, e-learning can't offer the interactions among participants that a classroom can. Face-to-face instruction is required at times. He said that the instructors initially were fearful that their jobs were going to be taken away if e-learning was utilized. The corporation spent time reassuring their instructors that this technology would actually be an aide to them in the classrooms, that it was not an either-or choice any longer. They spent time getting instructors to understand the usefulness of e-learning technology and appreciate the role that it could play in their own classroom environment.

Content/Design

IBM calls for subject-matter experts to verify the relevance of content and context. They follow the good principles of Web design and adult learning to make e-learning intuitive, engaging, and interactive. IBM places great sensitivity on cultural differences in designing their e-learning courses. With over 300,000 employees working in different parts of the world,

IBM has a serious challenge to maintain a single culture and yet be sensitive to local needs. They also need to be concerned about maintaining the corporate culture when they constantly gain so many outside employees from mergers and acquisitions. The designers will take cultural implications and the differences in requirements across different geographies to make appropriate cultural adaptations.

Another corporation I examined uses standardization and applies a layered approach using the commonalities as the first layer and superimposing additional layers to meet the needs of local organizations. Courses are stratified into layers and translated into 15 different languages.

Another corporation I examined uses interactivity and simulations so that it is not just text or images that are thrown across to the learners. The designers also include humor as another key ingredient. Culturally appropriate universal humor is very effective, as long as it is done in a professional way. In order to manage the expectation of the students, the designers said it is important to indicate the amount of time expected to complete a course. They make content design as rich as they can so people are engaged. They don't want students to feel short changed. They don't want students to view e-learning as just a cheap way of doing training. Many curriculum developers and instructors come from the technical world. They've worked on the technical side of business. For instructors who are not subject-matter experts, the designers work very closely with the subject-matter experts in developing the content. They also make it easier to create courses by giving the developer the ability to compile a list of preexisting learning objects. A learning object is a stand-alone piece of content that could be integrated with other pieces of content to form a course. A course designer, or developer, can specify what learning objects are required and in what sequence to develop a course on a particular subject matter. In order to keep the audience engaged, the learning modules should be short, discrete modules. For instance, if there is a class with five sets of classes that are two 8-hour days each, it's important to keep it engaging so that the material will keep the audience interested. The ideal length of a class is two to three hours per module. Eight hours is just too long. Developers should also avoid lengthy page-turners. A learning section should not be something that is 70 pages long before getting to the next section. In a long segment, after a while, trainees' eyes just glaze over. Each section should have no more than five to seven pages of text. This yardstick refers to synchronous Web class, which provides a live instructor. For asynchronous self-study, they recommend a 30-minute module length.

Cultural Sensitivity

With over 300,000 employees working in different parts of the world, it's a serious challenge to maintain a single culture and yet be sensitive to local needs. IBM has done an excellent job of creating a global learning community. The designers will take cultural implications and the differences in requirements across different geographies into consideration when making appropriate cultural adaptations.

Another company I examined also makes its curriculum adaptable to its global audience. That means the curriculum has to be easily translatable. If not, it will be costly to translate from one language to another because of the text or graphic layout.

Learner Consideration

IBM is sensitive to the ability and comfort of their target learner audience. It recognizes that people have different levels of technical competence and have different levels of willingness to accept e-learning. IBM acknowledges that currently people are more accustomed to being trained in classrooms, so e-learning is a major challenge. IBM places heavy emphasis on high touch. They recognize that people need to interact with people. Consequently, rich content and interactivity are important considerations in their design. If there's no high touch, high tech alone will not work. Most people want to talk to people, so, the goal is to figure out how they can best talk to people.

Another corporation I examined has an approach to meet learners at their levels of skills and knowledge. If that means designing a course at the eighth-grade comprehension level, they will do that. E-learning courses are available to employees on a 24/7 basis through the learning management system. Professional employees are generally well versed in technology. Many of the hourly workers don't have access to a laptop or a desktop, so they accommodate them with equipment and time in the plant or facility.

Another corporation I examined said that technical difficulties pose the greatest problem for users. Lack of bandwidth or proper equipment configuration will turn students off. Poor software navigation can also be a source of frustration. For example, if the developer uses flash video movies, but creates no capability of stopping or rewinding those movies, that would be a tedious and frustrating experience for a user. If the user missed a piece of information and needed to go back, he or she would have to restart the movie entirely, and it may take another 5 or 10 minutes to get back to the part that was missed. Technical consistency is also important. For example, if flash movies have a set of controls that allows the user to fast forward, rewind, stop, or play movie, those controls should be available in all the flash movies in the learning set, otherwise the user would be frustrated. Although there is still a high preference for classroom instruction over e-learning, the savings and efficiency that e-learning brings to the company cannot be denied. For example, it doesn't make sense to send 10 to15 people to a two-hour upgrade class. More and more, people are recognizing that it's not an either or situation, but that there are appropriate applications for each of the learning approaches. Whether it's classroom learning or e-learning, the ultimate goal is for the learner to learn the material and translate it into improvement in work performance.

Delivery

IBM recognizes the importance of the right delivery system. This means having the right infrastructure and having the right bandwidth to transmit the information to learners. IBM says that technical hurdles can derail e-learning quickly because a dissatisfied user just will not come back. IBM said navigation designs are an integral part of the delivery vehicle.

Another corporation I examined finds that technical difficulty is the biggest hurdle to e-learning. A senior learning leader from that corporation said that in terms of the set of negative comments that she gets, technology turnoff is one of the biggest. She explained that with the generation her corporation now has coming through, if an e-learning interface doesn't come back in 10 seconds, they are clicking off, because everyone's used to the Internet now. Nobody seems to want to wait 20 seconds for a screen to come on. A senior learning technology leader explained that you get into the whole issue of the servers and the infrastructure and how well they are performing. When a course isn't working, the training people run to the IT people and frequently they don't understand SCORM and all of those protocols and requirements.

Another corporation I examined has a chief e-learning architect who said that compatibility in the computer system is important. For example, Java version 1.14 is not compatible with all course work. The same is true for versions 1.13 or 1.12 or 1.11. Courses require a minimum screen resolution of 800 × 600, and there may still be people out there with a 640 × 480 screen. If the course doesn't display correctly, it will be perceived as something wrong with the course. If this is not tracked prior to launching the course, and the user is not informed that his connection speed may be low, the user will be frustrated. If user capability is not identified up front and his expectations not managed, the user will not come back.

Blended Learning

IBM is a proponent of doing prework via e-learning so that all participants come to the in-class courses starting on the same page. IBM believes that blended learning is the way to combine the best features of e-learning and classroom learning. IBM's Basic Blue is an excellent example of a blended learning approach. Its design includes getting the basic knowledge online prior to face to face session.

Another corporation I examined has a chief e-learning architect who said that blended learning is combining the best features of e-learning and classroom learning. He explained that learners can sit in the classroom or take an online course and learn how to fly a plane—but it doesn't mean they can fly a plane. They must step out of that classroom and get in a plane with an instructor to prove they can fly a plane; and that's the same concept that his corporation follows. In management education now, typically, a blended approach will be used; a person will do prework online followed by a face-to-face classroom session. More often than not, there will also be a six-month postresidential phase that will have students work on an actual learning project. It will be Web-based or Web-mediated or e-mail-mediated continuous learning.

Sourcing

IBM is willing to purchase standard, off-the-shelf courses that are often cheaper than its own products. It will also develop its own programs if there are unique circumstances or if external vendors are not capable of doing the work.

Another corporation I examined said that the decision to build versus buy depends on what's available in the marketplace. If it's a standard course, it may be more feasible to buy from the market. Compatibility of technology may be another important consideration. Another key consideration is to fully understand the needs assessment. If vendors are not clear about the needs, a great deal of time and money can be wasted without getting a useful product. There are hundreds of vendors to choose from when it comes to getting content and getting training management systems. Therefore, it's important to develop criteria to evaluate vendors in a systematic manner. Common templates and criteria with same rating scales will be useful for assessing vendor quality and streamlining the evaluation process. If a course is unique, the corporation will build it.

Another corporation I examined hires programmers out of school and designs and develops many of its own programs because these programs are not available in the marketplace. If the corporation already has preexisting content and the time is short, sometimes it will will build the courses for the requesting business unit within the corporation. It depends on where the corporation is , how far along and what its time restrictions are.

How Is E-Learning Implemented?

Marketing

IBM made e-learning voluntary at the initial phase of their e-learning program. They believe it is an important way to get early acceptance. Because people like to interact with people particularly at the early stages of e-learning experience, IBM also provides tutors in learning centers. In addition, they promptly follow up on requests on technical or content questions from learners.

Another corporation I examined encourages employees to use e-learning immediately in a course. The corporation explains the core competencies that people need to be successful in their roles or in roles they may aspire to.

Another corporation I examined indicated that the demand for e-learning increased substantially after 9/11. They restricted travel to some areas and eliminated travel to other areas. People were very tentative about traveling, so they became receptive to the use of a new medium that they were not accustomed to. There were also many financial cutbacks, so it became more cost efficient for people to start to use e-learning. Getting acceptance within the company was a two-prong attack. They had to overcome some technical difficulties and philosophical hurdles in getting groups to accept the use of e-learning. Asking students to give up travel and persuading them that instructor-led learning was not the only way were difficult tasks. To gain acceptance, the corporation's strategy was not to push the training on employees but to make it all voluntary and then communicate success stories to others. They used a pull, not a push method. They let students know that there were no strings attached and that e-learning was right there for them to better themselves. For the first two years, the company didn't make a single course mandatory. The company just built the courses and encouraged employees to go through the experience. The voluntary approach was largely a success, and the company soon reached the 50 percent penetration level in the enterprise. At that point, it was able to start to introduce a few mandatory courses via e-learning. Every single request is followed up quickly and communicated back to the person making the recommendation. This approach was used to make their students feel that the system built was theirs, because the corporation acted on their requests, and made sure it communicated to them afterwards.

Support Learners

IBM provides a learning management system with a learning portal where courses can be accessed and the history of learning can be obtained. It has help desks and e-mail systems to respond to problems that learners may encounter. It also takes the nature of the target audience into consideration. It maintains confidentiality of information. IBM also has an administrative support system for learners. For example, for the Basic Blue program, the administrator will monitor the learner's progress and follow up routinely to make sure that the precourse work is completed prior to the face-to-face sessions.

Another corporation I examined gives their employees access so they can go into the LMS to see the course catalog and the course development plans. This access will automatically provide employees with their learning history. It will list the history of courses that they have taken throughout their careers. Users can search for different functional areas such as career development, corporate programs, customer service, environmental, health and safety (EHS), finance, leadership and manufacturing. When users go into LMS, they can also access help through the central site, which hosts a community of experts from different disciplines. Users can ask questions and someone will get back to them. If it's a technical problem, the help desk will get the student through it; creating an environment conducive to e-learning helps the learner as well. The chief information officer said that they've given out signs that say, "E-Learning, Do Not Disturb."

Another corporation I examined said that employees who are not computer literate can stop by any of the learning centers scattered across the United States for some help in getting started with e-learning. Hands-on training is handled in their training centers and is normally a part of a blended learning curriculum. E-learning is available for 100 percent of their employees 24/7. Prior to the use of the LMS it was very hard for associate employees to access the Web. They were a difficult audience to reach by nature of their physical work environment and the demands of their workday. With the introduction of the LMS, employees have had the ability to access e-learning from outside the firewall. As a result, there has been a surge of participation activity on the part of their associates. It's simply learning that goes on after hours. These are people who cannot access online learning during the day because their jobs just don't permit it.

Lack of Time Allocation for E-Learning

Although management philosophy is to provide time for doing e-learning during work hours, in practice, this is often difficult for employees to do because of their heavy workloads and busy schedules, so they often end up doing e-learning at night or on weekends. This is the case for IBM. For example, for IBM's Basic Blue program, management's intent is to set time aside for e-learning, but the reality is that managers are more apt to do e-learning on their own time rather than taking two hours off to do e-learning during work. If they took off two hours during the day, they would end up working their regular job at night. The job simply doesn't go away. IBM employees readily accept and understand that this training may take them into late evenings or weekends. Work-life balance is a challenge that they face. They understand that it's not a nine-to-five job. Ted Hoff, the CLO, acknowledged that this is an issue that runs counter to what they have been saying about encouraging learning. This is an issue that IBM needs to address and find feasible ways to carve out time and space during work hours.

Another corporation I examined said that setting aside time for e-learning has been a challenge. In spite of all the best intentions, people just can't find that time to do it during working hours. People are already working long hours, so learning generally takes place during off hours.

Another corporation I examined said that management employees' time is their own as long as they get their work done. In other words, employees could sit at their desks and take courses if they want to, but they are still responsible for meeting the work deadlines. For nonsalaried employees, supervisor approval is required, but if they don't get supervisor's approval, the employees can still access e-learning as long as they get their work done. However, if the work isn't completed because they were taking courses without supervisor's approval, then they must be responsible for the consequences of their actions.

Confidentiality

At IBM, the various personal feedbacks on e-learning are visible on the Web, but the details are not released to the manager or anybody else. Managers simply need to know that an individual passed a required course, rather than know the score or how many times the individual took the test.

Another corporation I examined said that it also deals with data privacy. In the past, learning was not necessarily thought of as a very sensitive point, but with visibility of information in the e-learning space, the corporate learning staff is careful not to take gender, race, and other sensitive information from their HR software. A learning technology leader explained that there is also the issue of test scores. Did you pass with a 75? Did you pass with 100? How can test takers' desire for confidentiality be protected? Learning online is great, but then these sensitive issues crop up. With e-learning, training and development professionals want to understand how long users were in there taking the test, and some courses are designed to be taken only a given number of times.

Another corporation I examined said that confidentiality is increasingly becoming an issue in the e-learning space. Scores on tests are kept confidential and are not released to supervisors. The logic is that if someone is trying to improve his or her life by improving skills, the last thing he or she wants is to have his or her supervisor know that he or she has a failing score. The employee may be more valuable to the corporation by going to another position or he or she may perform well and realize his or her full potential. The employee is going through this process on his or her own time. Confidentiality will maintain the employee's trust. Once trust is lost, it's very difficult to regain it.

Support Instructors

IBM recognizes that e-learning instructors face a greater challenge in keeping the audience engaged, much more so than the classroom instructors. E-learning requires a very different set of skills than classroom teaching. In the classroom, the instructor is teaching a class with the view of the entire class. In the e-learning world, the instructor is facilitating discussion without seeing the audience. In this situation, the instructor has to be much more aggressive in eliciting interactions. The instructor may not be the subject-matter expert but instead is just facilitating a discussion. IBM provides training for instructors. IBM trains its instructors to be sensitive to the audience and be much more aggressive in eliciting interactions in e-learning situations.

Another corporation I examined has a senior learning leader who said that being an instructor in the e-learning world is a challenge, particularly if the instructor is more used to teaching in a face-to-face environment. It takes a lot of energy from the instructional standpoint. The curriculum needs to be highly interactive. The instructors generally have to be more aggressive to bring out interactivity. The biggest challenge for instructors is to learn how to use the tools that help them disseminate their information. And in synchronous training, instructors have to learn the tools, how to ask questions, and how to help people log on. Instructors are given training in adult learning and how to run an e-learning class. At one business unit, instructors are routinely given training in adult-learning techniques. They are also trained in virtual training. They also spend time learning how best to deliver an effective presentation in a virtual classroom that has been prepared by outside vendors. Tag team is another approach that helps e-learning instructors. Instructors found that teaching in teams of two where one instructor was advancing the slides and the other instructor was doing the narration, was ideal. Tag-team teaching seemed to work really well on the Web, because one person can pay attention to teaching and the other can just listen and handle technical issues.

Another corporation I examined has trainers who are trained upfront to engage the audience in a Web class. Instructors are given three classes. The first class covers the basics of e-learning protocols. The second covers the Web class delivery techniques. The third class teaches them to work with the PowerPoint presentations. Training will help the instructor to be successful with the class and avoid users having a bad experience resulting in their telling others to avoid e-learning. Instructors should be involved in curriculum development. There are many new methods that are used in online content creation. The chief e-learning architect said that teachers are by nature avid learners. There is no better way to learn something than to have to teach it, and if the instructor is always teaching different subjects, he or she will become an expert on those different subjects regardless of whether he or she has taught them before. Instructors are just natural learners. They will be partners in this process. However, e-learning is a huge shift for an instructor. Classroom instructors are used to being in the center of the audience and in control of the whole situation. E-learning takes a teacher away from the center and sits the teacher on the side. The e-learning teacher is basically fielding questions from students learning on their own and then is helping students prove their competency. Therefore, it's often a difficult transition for instructors to shift from the classroom to the e-learning environment. For a Web class, from one senior instructor's viewpoint, it's just between her and the microphone. Anybody can log in from anywhere, so people in Dallas, Fort Wayne, or Tampa, can log on and she can have a full class of students, each with a headset. They can raise their hands, and get the microphone. It's very hard after being an instructor looking at a class full of faces to not know if users are understanding her. The instructor has to be much more animated in a Web class to make sure the audience understands her. The instructor has to constantly ask questions, entertain the audience to make sure they are engaged. It's difficult for some instructors because they are talking to a faceless audience and they don't even know what the audience is thinking about. The reality is that some instructors will be lost in the conversion process, others will excel.

However, e-learning is useful when you have to reach a large number of people in a large geographic landscape. The new challenge and excitement to the instructor is the ability to reach so many people at once. Each learning situation has different challenges and different opportunities. Personal satisfaction has to be defined differently. The chief e-learning architect said that he helped train 13,000 people, whereas, before e-learning, he could only train 20. He gets tremendous satisfaction out of it. E-learning is also proven to be extremely successful from the standpoint that people don't have to wait for a whole classroom to fill up. Students can access training immediately. For example, before e-learning, if you had 7 technicians and you needed 12 to fill a classroom, the class would not be scheduled. Now the class can take place immediately.

Corporate Support

IBM provides a tremendous amount of support to their employees for learning. IBM spends about $1 billion on learning. They have a strong learning culture. People know that their opportunities and careers are dependent on the merits of their performance.

Another corporation I examined has a CLO who said that it is most important for a corporation to have a culture that encourages people to learn, and to hire and promote people who are always improving themselves. People will want to learn in this type of environment because they are motivated by the corporation supporting their learning process. As a part of their learning culture, employees constantly demand more learning opportunities. It was just not feasible to provide all training in a face-to-face manner because of high costs and time away from work. So there was a good deal of acceptance of e-learning from employees because they wanted to learn more and learn faster. Their culture is one of change and adaptability. A senior learning leader explained that it's not a place where employees can get comfortable and say that they know all there is to know about this kind of database, so they will have a job for the next 20 years. This senior learning leader said that she could almost guarantee that that would not happen. Their culture is based very strongly around a meritocracy.

Another corporation I examined has a CLO who said that the corporation took an organic approach to how people use e-learning. From the start, the company did not set hard and fast rules about access to online learning during the normal workday for management employees. The company's employees also had access to online learning outside the workday. The company introduced its LMS, which provides a common platform that allows users to access courses from behind the firewall, so if users are at work, they go through the normal company network. They can also get access from outside the firewall. They can do it at night, on the weekend, 3:00 in the morning, and the like. The company has sophisticated software that interrogates not only their desktop computer suitability for the learning (i.e., correct plug-ins) but also tracks the time a learner spends on e-learning. The company intended not to set any rules, but it does monitor the usage patterns. The results over the last several years have been interesting. Typically, users log on before 8 A.M. and after 4 P.M. in the afternoon. The company observed a predictable spike in the 11 A.M. to 1 P.M. range, which is typically a period of time when people would be at lunch. The company also sees interesting patterns with respect to days of the week. Tuesday is the most active day. Other days are falling off. Since the introduction of LMS, utilization has increased after 6:00 P.M. at night and on the weekends. The company also established a centralized support hotline for the Web class. Their development interns and software developers handle the support calls for the Web class.

Learning Management System

IBM has an LMS that provides interoperability and a common platform for various parts of their companies to share information. IBM's Lotus LMS handles instructor-led and online training for its global community and covers more than 30 languages. It's a platform used to train its employees, customers, suppliers, and business partners (Donovan 2003). IBM has a collaborative space whereby information can be shared among employees.

Another corporation I examined has a single LMS with one platform for scheduling, managing, and delivering e-learning activities. The LMS provides a single point of entry for employees to access courses, access completion records, and search for support information. The corporation has a set of guidelines with technical specifications for courseware to be launched and to take advantage of recording, tracking, and other information. Several years ago, the company struggled to communicate because they had multiple learning systems. They had about 20 different LMSs that were being used across the company. A senior learning leader said that one of the best examples that people use when they talk about LMS involves the point at which they first got started with e-mail in the company. They had several different e-mail platforms, so it was difficult to communicate. Now they have a single e-mail platform. They also have an internal Web site, which includes thousands of communities of people with common knowledge in specific areas such as aircraft engines, plastics, and marketing. It's their electronic black book. Each community has experts and facilitators. Each represents a knowledge-sharing tool that allows knowledge to be transferred to one another. The participation is completely voluntary, so anyone can create a community on any topic that he or she wants. It's self-motivated. The company has thousands of communities. It's their largest online activity.

Another corporation I examined built its own LMS, which provides a single portal or gate to e-learning. When building an LMS, the first priority must be availability of bandwidth in the enterprise. Potential data bottlenecks need to be identified and addressed prior to deployment. The second priority is to have a talented technical staff to serve as intermediary between vendors and users. The third priority is to be prepared for technical support. If support is not provided immediately, some employees that may want to take courses voluntarily will be lost. The fourth priority is to partner with service and product providers. It is also necessary to have regular meetings and review successes and failures. Deploying and managing an enterprise LMS should be viewed as a long learning process.

How Is Effectiveness Determined by Corporations?

IBM uses levels 1 to 4 of the Kirkpatrick model for measuring the effectiveness of e-learning. They measure learners' feedbacks, mastery of the skills, applications of those skills, avoided travel costs, and productivity savings. They follow the same model but vary in the extent of the application of the Kirkpatrick model. The bottom line is that there always has to be a business case for doing e-learning. It has to make sense from a strategic and financial prospective. IBM measures every level of the e-learning process. Level 1 is a survey of users' reaction to a course. For Basic Blue, based on 11,000 respondents, the feedback was 1.02 on a scale of 1 to 5, with1 being the top rating. IBM gets feedback from participants of the courses and the facilitators. Based on the feedback over the first two years, there were more than 300 changes made to the Basic Blue program. On level 2, there are some requisite skills or knowledge that need to be mastered in many courses. If students pass the mastery test, then they are ready to build upon that basic knowledge in the face-to-face module. On level 3, they measure the application of what's learned in the class. That is, how does the learner transfer learning to the job and is there change in behavior? For Basic Blue, a survey is done six months after the completion of the program to see if there are some differences in performance. On level 4, IBM deals with the calculation of savings associated with e-learning. The savings result from a number of factors: shorter time in covering the same content, avoided travel costs and associated expenses, and potential productivity savings that could be achieved if e-learning resulted in a more efficient way of doing work. Although the development cost of e-learning is a lot more expensive than the traditional classroom instructor-led course, the increased development cost is just a one-time expense. In a traditional class, every time new people come in, more cost is being incurred. IBM's effectiveness measurements go beyond the Kirkpatrick model. IBM applies the accountability, content, and effectiveness (ACE) model, which measures external customer satisfaction. This is a way to correlate learners' satisfaction from learning with their improved performance. Their improved performance translates to more satisfied customers, which leads to greater revenues for the company. IBM's goal is to generate revenues and maximize profits, so measuring customer satisfaction is the ultimate way of linking e-learning to business objectives. According to Lau, the Kirkpatrick model is more focused on the learning event itself and its effectiveness. That effectiveness measurement includes increased knowledge, application of knowledge, and impact of knowledge on the business. However, the learning might affect the customer interface as well. The additional impact is whether the customer is satisfied with the service.

Another corporation I examined tracks usage of both mandatory and voluntary courses. The bulk of the courses conducted by this corporation are voluntary, and for this category, the greater emphasis is placed on measuring usage instead of savings. Voluntary e-learning provides a venue for people who want to learn about something, for self-improvement or a work situation. In required courses, the focus is on how many students can be processed within a certain amount of time. Time is an important element when it comes to being able to reach employees across the globe. In mandatory courses, calculations on instructor utilization, cost savings, and cost avoidance are done. According to a senior learning leader, for those courses that are voluntary, although the company may monitor some cost savings, the larger focus is on usage and making sure that people are aware of the courses and using them. It is important to make sure that people are not going to other places to use other training that's more expensive. That's the whole rationale. This senior learning leader said that she hoped that somebody's not walking down the street to a live Java class, but that they would get Java II skills in the corporation's e-learning library. Completion rate is different for mandatory and voluntary courses. For compliance reasons, EHS courses are required and they are measured very closely. The corporation is constantly sending out reminders. These courses are mandatory so they get completed, but what about courses that are optional? This is a harder task because people have to be convinced that these courses are good for their skills development even though they are voluntary. For example, this senior learning leader asked, why aren't people using the HR tech course that is offered? The managers have to understand and be convinced of the value of it from a professional development perspective. If they want to have a competency level for their sales individuals, this course helps manage that process for them. A learning leader remarked that there's a lot of work they need to do inside their organization to educate people about how they can use this tool to manage competencies. So completion rate for mandatory courses should be differentiated from voluntary courses. Another challenge is trying to figure out whether users just take the test without really going through the subject matter.

Digitizing content also means compression of training time, which leads to substantial savings. According to a learning leader, for one business unit, the amount of compression could easily be 50, 60, and 70 percent and as high as 80 percent. For savings calculations, she said that she used 40 percent, which was a conservative estimate. When asked how the savings calculation is done, she explained, that basically, the company figured it was reducing the amount of time it was taking employees off the job, and it used $30 per hour and the company had 92,000 units, which was one person, one course, and it had an average course length of a little over two hours. The company figured it could bring that length down by 40 percent and just multiplied out. According to a learning leader, this is how the company made their business case.

In another corporation I examined, the chief e-learning architect defines three broad categories of measurements for determining effectiveness of e-learning. These include cultural acceptance, financial impact, and soft measures. Cultural acceptance reflects general acceptance of e-learning among students. It addresses such issues as attendance, type of audience, and general acceptance. Cultural acceptance is deemed to be critical to success in e-learning. Financial impact is the savings resulting from e-learning. It addresses issues such as cost avoidance, revenue generation, and efficiency. Financial impact must be measured against the appropriate benchmark. That benchmark could be instructor-led training or others or oneself. Soft measurement is the third category, and it includes retention, morale, and other qualities that are difficult to measure. According to the chief e-learning architect, the notion of anytime, anywhere availability is not useful if no one comes to use e-learning. As a way to encourage acceptance, e-learning was started as voluntary, not mandatory, learning. Early adopters were provided with quick feedback to generate enthusiasm and acceptance. For example, their questions were responded to within one business day, and they were immediately informed when their suggestions were acted upon. Students, of course, can write in their comments anytime. By making early adopters become an integral part of the developmental process, they were able to use them as champions to spread the gospel of e-learning. They use an online evaluation system, which is integrated into their LMS to routinely evaluate the learner's postclass experience. The traditional Kirkpatrick level-one (customer survey) and level-two (mastery tests) evaluations are done and tracked automatically.

Customer survey is a simple tool used to gauge the users' reactions to courseware, design and usefulness of e-learning. Surveys used typically include a series of statements, and users are asked to rank each category from one to five, with five being the highest score. Typical statements are as follows: It was easy to access this course; My work environment supports this type of learning; I had the skills and/or knowledge required to start this course; The equipment required for this course was functioning properly (computer, keyboard, mouse, etc); The system responded quickly; It was easy to navigate through this course (I knew what to do and when to do it); It was easy to track my progress throughout the course; The audio/video/animation was clear and to the point; The way this course was delivered (such as CD-ROM, Web-based, video) was an effective way for me to learn this subject; I clearly understood the course objectives; The course content was logically organized; The course used language I could understand; The practice exercises helped me learn the course content; The practice exercises provided helpful feedback; My skills and/or knowledge increased as a result of this course; I will have the opportunity to use what was taught in this course back on the job; I will be able to apply the skills and or knowledge taught in the course back on the job; I intend to use at least some of the skills and or knowledge taught in this course back on the job; I will be using what was taught in this course to further my career development opportunities outside of my current position; Overall I was satisfied with this course.

Whether a course is mandatory or voluntary also makes a difference in completion rate. The company hasn't set any hard and fast rules, because e-learning is primarily voluntary and not mandatory. When a course is mandatory, the completion is quite high. For example, the code of business ethics course, a 30-minute online module, which every management employee must take, will yield 100 percent completion. The course will generate a high rate of completion because it is a company-mandated learning experience. Those kinds of mandated learning experiences are few and far between. Most of the draw to e-learning is organic employee behavior. Therefore, if a company has a high completion rate, it may mean there is a greater amount of company mandate. That may explain why that company's numbers are what they are compared to another company with numbers that are largely the result of voluntary employee behavior. The company has taken the approach of letting learner behavior operate by itself. Hence the company mandated learning has been minimal. The chief learning officer reflected that it caused them over the last couple of years to become much wiser in how they look at access hours, at completion rates, loiter time and all those things, not in terms of what's good or bad, but in terms what kind of the natural behavior of learners in this kind of an environment.

Another measure of effectiveness is called performance linkage. It is done much more with grass-roots technical learning. For example, a class of newly hired technicians is being trained for an outside plant course. It's a blended course with time for online training and then time for going out to do hands-on practice. If 12 people graduated from the course in Monrovia, California, then the company will track the performance of those 12 people over the course of the next 180 days. The tracking is done through an online system. The supervisor who does the normal postcourse assessment will assess each employee after 30 days, 60 days, 90 days, and 180 days to see how well each is doing the job. That information will be entered into a database. The tracking can be done on a real-time basis to determine who is performing well. If nine people are performing well and three are faltering in their role, the company has the ability to go to the diagnosis to determine whether the students' deficits are related to the original learning experience. So if there's something that students didn't master, the company can go back and take a look at how the instructor rated them. It can go back and take a look at the parts of students' learning where they struggled. The company can do some root cause analysis, and it can also take a look at whether there were some environmental factors that might be influencing the deficiencies in performance. Perhaps students are working in a neighborhood in Los Angeles where there is heavy traffic and instead of getting six jobs per day done, they're only getting four jobs per day done simply because they're spending part of the day locked up in traffic. The company can go back and tie those findings to the instructor who had them in class. This is an innovation that has come along in the last 12 to 18 months, and it goes way beyond the survey response. Instead, it relates the learning experience directly to how the individual is performing on the job. In the last year, the company used this approach in eight or nine major job categories. It is now able to track the performance of the learner over a period of time after the learning experience. The company can also diagnose the specific deficit so it doesn't have to send a person back for the whole learning experience, when, in fact, all the student needs is a two hour module to get the refresher training that is needed.

In selected cases, the company will also look into organizational metrics such as revenues, income, and customer service. It will go all the way up to Kirkpatrick Level 4 evaluation. It will do the analysis in a very systematic and comprehensive way and typically reserve that type of evaluation for special cases because of the time and expense involved. It reserves that evaluation for interventions that had front-end expectations that there would be an ROI associated with them.

The key components of financial analysis include the following: e-learning cost = (licensing fees + content development costs + courseware integration costs + courseware maintenance costs + amortized IT infrastructure cost + support cost); attendance cost = (number of students that would have attended an instructor-led course if e-learning tools were not available × (average hourly salary × time spent in training)); delivery cost = ((instructor average hourly salary × length of each training session) × number of training sessions necessary to train the number of students referred to in attendance cost); travel cost = cost savings based on the elimination of commuting and travel for the people mentioned in attendance cost; increased revenue = increased net revenue due to increased customer-facing time. The resulting formula for cost savings is as follows:

$$\text{Savings} = \text{e-learning cost} - (\text{attendance cost} + \text{delivery cost} + \text{travel cost} + \text{increased revenue}).$$

Proving productivity would literally require someone to follow the student around. Unless the student is a factory worker doing one task, such as stamping seven cars instead of five, there are other contributing factors to productivity levels. For example, if an employee is supposed to be driving a truck and fixing wires, but couldn't get anywhere because there was 24 inches of snow, this lack of productivity has nothing to do with the employee's ability. Therefore, the difficulty lies in isolating a single factor of e-learning. Unless there is a tightly focused control study (e.g., sales people), and one group of sales people gets training and the other group does not, and all other conditions are identical, it's difficult to measure the impact of a single factor. If a student attends a programming course, how does one measure the benefit? Should the student be assigned to the same job that he or she did last month to see how much more quickly he or she gets it done? This is not practical, because he or she has already finished what was needed to be done last month and has moved on to something new. The world is not cut and dry, and it is difficult to hold the environment constant. Even the avoided travel cost is disputable. Students are asked whether they would have taken training elsewhere and traveled to another to location to receive training if the training were not available online. Sampling the population is a way to estimate percentages and apply them to savings calculations.

One important observation made by the CLO is that although the number of visits to and loitering time within e-learning seem to be increasing, the completion rate for e-learning courses has stayed relatively constant in recent times. The CLO suggested that there might be a new paradigm developing, and consequently, the completion rate may not be the right measure to assess the level of participation and effectiveness in e-learning. Because e-learning courses are built from modular blocks, learners may just be going in to learn the portion of the course that's needed. This may be more effective e-learning rather than less. The chief e-learning architect explained that it's not the completion rate that matters but rather how e-learning affects business performance. He said that the trick is to understand business objectives and map the training to those specific objectives. Loitering time may in fact be real learning time. This is an issue that the company investigated further to determine what the effective way of measuring completion in the e-learning world was. To start, a series of focus-group sessions was conducted to understand the reasons behind learners' behavior toward the use of e-learning. Can controlled experiments and self-reporting feedbacks be used to understand the patterns of e-learning behavior? Can courses be further divided into smaller slices? In e-learning space, access and completion may be two very different things. The company made the observation that people exhibit very different behavior when they come into the e-learning space.

What Lessons Are Learned?

E-learning failure can occur because of technical difficulties, poor quality of content, lack of corporate support, and lack of learner motivation. IBM and other corporations found that technical difficulties such as bandwidth and browser incompatibility, constrained learners' access to e-learning. IBM found that learners don't have time to do e-learning during work hours but do e-learning mostly during off hours. IBM found that it is very important not to assume learners' receptivity to e-learning and to maintain high touch.

Failure at the Learner Level

IBM found technical difficulties to be a major deterrent. For example, IBM pointed out that when e-learning is being applied, it must be relevant and focused for the target audience. It found that just having a lot of courses on the Web doesn't mean that the company is providing anything that's really valuable. IBM pointed out that people realized that that was not effective learning. It is also important to understand the nature of the target audience and to recognize the level of human touch required in a learning program. For example, when IBM was hiring a lot of people in Asia, they assumed that because India is high-tech, that e-learning would take place faster in India. They assumed that these people learned English and are technically literate, and thus they would gravitate to e-learning more easily than Americans. That was not the case because the users needed to talk to human beings at some point.

Another corporation I examined said that multitasking is a distraction to e-learning. It is important to get people to understand that they are not going to learn anything if they are going to multitask. If they are doing e-learning, they should avoid taking conference calls, doing instant messaging, e-mailing, and other distractions. They should be committed to this e-learning session for the duration of the course. In the e-learning world, the instructor already has a difficult task in keeping the class engaged. The instructor has to be much more dynamic in the virtual environment to keep the audience interested. Multitasking will make it even harder for the instructor to get the message across to learners.

Another corporation I examined noted that the main difficulties were technical difficulties and accepting e-learning as an alternate way of learning. Because its employees are working in the telecommunications industry, one would have expected them to have fewer technical difficulties because they deal with the latest routers, wireless networks, and PCs. Nonetheless, many employees do run into difficulties, so as a first step, the instructors are briefed on how to get everybody comfortable with PCs. As a first technical requirement, e-learning must be accompanied with sufficient bandwidth; otherwise, students get frustrated because there is either no response or the response rate is too slow. The students must also have the proper software so they can use the application at hand. For example, they must have the appropriate flash plug-in installed in their Web browser. Numerous technical difficulties can stop learners in their tracks, so tracking mechanisms were built into their LMS. The company collects over 200 technical specifications for an end user's PC. When these are logged into their LMS, end users will be matched against course requirements. If there are any discrepancies, end users will be guided through the resolution. For example, if users are taking a course that requires a flash plug-in of a particular version, they will quickly be able to determine if the PC is equipped with the capability to log into the course. If users don't have the flash plug installed, the program will let them know what they need to do to install it. According to the chief e-learning architect, for example, some folks don't know what a flash plug-in is. They click on a course, wanting to take it, and they're actually showing initiative and interest, but all of a sudden the PC doesn't connect for them. When that happens, they don't come back. However, if you manage users' expectations—if they are informed that they need to install a flash plug-in or that they have a very slow network connection, and the course may run slowly—they'll be more tolerant. They'll then come back next time.

Another area where lessons were learned was in bringing about change in the mindset of users about accepting e-learning as another means of learning and viewing it as a benefit to lifetime learning for the user. The company's organic approach to e-learning and its commitment to produce quality e-learning are key elements in bringing about acceptance to e-learning. For many students, taking a course away from an instructor-led training session and changing it to e-learning denies them a well-deserved break from work. The company has made sure that the students don't view e-learning as a cheap way of doing training but rather as an effective way of doing it.

Another challenge is to convince the students that e-learning facilitates lifetime learning because of availability and ease of access. Students should look upon it as similar to the tuition-refund program offered by the company. This is simply another way to provide another benefit to the employees to improve their skills.

Failure at the Product Level

IBM stated that the business objectives must be articulated up front and that content must be relevant and presented in the proper context. They recognize that e-learning doesn't apply to everything. The range of e-learning application goes from simple to complex. For example, IBM initially started by purchasing a large library of e-learning courses. It had thousands of courses on the Web, but a lot of people weren't using them because there was no focus. The bottom line is that e-learning has to be to put in the context of the job that someone's doing and it must address what changes are required. IBM also found that proper user engagement must be created. The ability of users to connect easily to the e-learning program is an important consideration. Poor user engagement could be a disaster. According to Nancy Lewis, Vice President of On Demand Learning, IBM encountered a big problem with user engagement when Basic Blue was first rolled out. Lewis said that the writing was brilliant, but this brilliance was dulled by all the instruction and care that had to be done to create workable user engagement. IBM actually made 800 changes on user engagement. IBM also noted that content must be of high quality. According to Weintraub, bad content could be a problem in the e-learning space because there is no instructor there to shift the focus of the class. The benefit of being in a classroom is that the instructor can change extemporaneously very easily to offset a poor design. It's harder to do so in an e-learning situation. The requirements for e-learning have to be established in a rigorous manner so that the audience is getting something they really need to know.

Another corporation I examined said that e-learning doesn't work for complex content because development of that content would be very costly. According to the CLO, advanced-level instruction is directed toward teaching someone a different way to diagnose the problem. It teaches different and unique perspectives. It looks at all the ingredients of knowledge, content, and skill of the individual to create the right solution. Face-to-face learning is most valuable when participants learn from one another.

Another corporation I examined said that failure of e-learning can occur if the content cannot be delivered or cannot be accessed and the content is not best suited for e-learning. The "e" part of e-learning is critical. Bandwidth is also critical, and should be widely available in the near future. Without sufficient bandwidth, the user will not be able to access software that requires greater bandwidth. E-learning is simply a new process for an old task. The chief e-learning architect explained that the only thing you really have to worry about is the technological part of e-learning. The bottom-line is that if the content is great and the technology is poor, the poor technology nullifies the content. If the content is poor and the technology works, the students may still get some margin of satisfaction. According to the chief e-learning architect, if the course needs a higher version of flash plug-in or whatever the application might be, he can direct the student to upgrade the software. Otherwise, the student will get to a particular page and call him and tell him that the course is broken.

Accessing the course can be another difficulty if the administrative rights are not given beforehand. For example, students are trying to attend a Web class and they're having a problem downloading the course. Problems could stem from not having the necessary administrative rights. Their LAN administrator might have locked down their desktop and they can't install any software or they just don't know how to run an application installer. A senior Web specialist explained that if you don't have the course installed, people just get hung up. Although the newer e-learning tools are more interactive and have more animations, it is still a challenge for designers to make sure the layout is engaging, students have ample opportunities to ask questions, and answers are provided to them immediately. The company uses adult-learning experts, designers, and developers to make sure that the best principles of content design are used for developing a computer-based training classes and Web classes. E-learning doesn't lend itself equally well to all applications. For example, it's more difficult to learn a programming language via e-learning than it is to learn how a tool works. The instruction of a programming language that has all the technical nuances may be better suited for classroom training. Programming has technicalities such as semicolons, curly brackets, and other concepts that are difficult to absorb. On the other hand, for instruction on how to use a tool, e-learning can be an excellent approach that will save the user the difficulty of reading through a complicated set of instructions in a manual and figuring out how to use this new tool.

Failure at Organizational Level

Management support is an important ingredient in implementing e-learning. The support comes in the form of investment in training programs, training employees, and dedicating time for employees to learn. IBM recognizes the challenge of e-learning to instructors and the importance of establishing partnerships with line organizations and IT departments. Ted Hoff said that lack of dedicated time for e-learning is a problem at IBM also. He explained that right now, when employees have any face-to-face learning, students are given the dedicated time but when it's pure e-learning, that often does not happen. If users are constantly thwarted when attempting to do e-learning, they will be discouraged. If the manager repeatedly interrupts e-learning, users will not try it anymore. At IBM, they also recognize that underestimating the challenge faced by e-learning instructors could be a problem. One of the mistakes that IBM made was in thinking that anybody who's a good teacher would do fine in an e-learning situation.

Another corporation I examined said that E-learning doesn't apply to everything. According to the chief learning officer, at the advanced level, instruction is directed toward teaching someone a different way to diagnose the problem. It teaches different and unique perspectives. It looks at all the ingredients of knowledge, content, and skill of the individual to create the right solution. In these situations, he explained that there was not one bit of content that was something they didn't know at all. It's all in a higher level of diagnosis and combining things they know for the unique solution. In these situations, a face-to-face approach is more feasible. It involves a much smaller population at an enormous cost. He said that there are very few complex situations in which it makes sense to use e-learning. One such example is the risk management course developed for the financial services unit. At the core is a small group of people that have to access every deal based on risk assessment, and it means hundreds of millions of dollars. That's something that's very complex and difficult. A small number of people take it and unit cost is enormous, but it's something that's necessary to develop that high level of expertise. Complex situations are all about interactions. At these levels, you have competent people. He said that you see the different dimensions and you learn from one another. That's the big value. People are learning from people. It's not people learning from machines.

Another corporation I examined said that corporate support is crucial for success in e-learning. Change is always difficult, and changing from traditional in-class learning to e-learning is no different. The company has done an excellent job in managing that change by communicating the benefits of e-learning and getting the buy-in from its employees. Corporate support means requiring major capital investment. It means developing e-learning expertise. It means cooperation among different organizations and working closely with the IT organization.

The company was challenged by a long tradition of instructor-led learning as the way they do things and as its preferred way of doing things. There is a great deal of imbedded infrastructure investment that supports that instructor-led teaching. They have people who are very set in their ways. Not just those instructors and developers and learning professionals, but also organizations and employees. Therefore, it is not easy to bring about a change to e-learning. The CLO explained that the company has had to spend a lot of time educating and socializing all those involved on the benefits of beginning to rethink that paradigm. The company has had to do it in a way that doesn't threaten anyone involved, that meets them where they are, and begins to introduce them to the benefits of expanding their approaches to learning beyond the instructor-led modality. Especially if they are used to the tradition of instructor-led learning, instructors are going to view e-learning as a threat. They're going to view it as a loss of prestige and status, and they have to be brought along to realize that this is another tool. Instructors have to be persuaded that they now have the power of very sophisticated tools to make them more effective as learning professionals. It's not a question of something being either instructor led or Web mediated. It's the question of what blend is needed. Is it a 90/10, 60/40, or 50/50 ratio? What's the ratio of e-mediated learning versus instructor-mediated learning? Depending on the contents and objectives, each learning experience will dictate a different recipe.

As to the company's LMS, the list of challenges it had to face was quite enormous, and it included dealing with thousands of locations, multiple Web browsers, and the integration of multiple vendor products. Most of the challenges were technical in nature, such as bandwidth, browser, and end-user workstation configurations. Initially, the company's technical support handled those issues that arose. With experience, the company began to identify some patterns and root causes. It began to write and license software to identify those potential issues at the point of login, then guide its end users through a self-service process of preventive support. Consequently the support calls decreased substantially. This allowed the company to repurpose its support staff, which was very familiar with their products and processes. The company also handled vendor product integration by working with the vendors. In the past, training content was developed and force fitted into the corporate LMS. As a result, most online courses were not in a standard format. Thus, an average of 80 labor hours was required to integrate a single course that was either created or modified. This was untenable because the resource requirements often exceeded existing resources. The company can have up to 40 courses in development at any given time. The need to republish these noncompliant courses into a single format became critical as their numbers increased, and the need to keep them updated was apparent. As a result, the company decided to standardize on the SCORM specification in order to reduce the time and effort required to integrate courses with the LMS. The investment in standards-based LMS has enabled it to respond quicker to changes in business needs. The adoption of the LMS enabled the content development group to standardize its e-learning development processes, which has also contributed to developer productivity. The company anticipates being able to further leverage its technology investment to begin reusing learning content. The chief e-learning architect said that the company estimates that developing a new course with no existing learning content takes 40 to 80 hours of development and costs from $15,000 to $30,000 per instructional hour. This estimate includes all costs for instructional design, project management, and outsourcing of content development. The two most common technical issues that discourage e-learners are low bandwidth and incorrect configurations. Bandwidth is the primary frustration, but incorrect browser and PC settings are the second most common cause of e-learner defection. Learners expecting a trouble-free learning environment can get discouraged when faced with technical difficulties. They may not come back. A course packed with full motion video and audio will require much more bandwidth than a course made up of mostly text and still images. A large course can take longer to load, and sometimes the audience thinks that the course is broken.

Another important lesson is the need to commit to e-learning as a major investment. E-learning can be costly and the projects launched should yield high ROI. Isolated and fragmented small projects will not yield the best results for the investment. The CLO explained that any organization that hasn't taken a serious plunge into e-learning, needs to resist the temptation to get caught up in the high school science project syndrome. In other words, if people have come to initiate great ideas and claim they need small seed money for projects, he believes they should be told to come up with serious business applications for e-learning that require a big commitment. A big commitment means one that's going to have a big payoff for telephone operations or wireless or government systems. It means getting out of a high school science project mentality of spending $10,000 here and $10,000 there. It means going to the line executives with propositions that are millions of dollars in terms of investment, but tens of millions of dollars in terms of potential returns either in savings of delivery, time, travel, and so forth. Further, concentrating investment in platform at the enterprise level makes a lot of sense. If investment decisions are left to lines of businesses with respect to building platforms or entering into enterprise wide content licenses from third party providers and vendors, there is a high risk of underutilizing investment, fragmenting corporate strategy, and at the end of the day facing disparate content and delivery mechanisms, none of which will be well integrated. The CLO explained that if you let that fragment, you're going to waste a lot of time, money, and effort, with very little to show for it.

Partnerships with business leaders are also essential, especially if the goal is to try to reshape the company's thinking about the nature of learning within the organization. If it's not done properly, turf battles will be created and more time will be spent on fixing those misunderstandings and disagreements than getting the job done. It is important to view the investment in the LMS in the context of enterprise IT strategy. For example, if your enterprise strategy is a Peoplesoft strategy or a systems, applications, and products (SAP) strategy, it's important to have a very early and important partnership formed with the IT community. They are the people who will be supporting the LMS, and who will be making sure that the decisions that you make as the learning professional with respect to e-learning are compatible with their long-term strategy relative to the IT environment. This partnership prevents e-learning professionals involved with LMS from going down one path only to find out six months later that the Peoplesoft and LMS that they just spent all this time building are not going to be compatible with this new direction. There's an advantage for e-learning professionals to have their own hip-pocket resources of IT professionals, but there is a need to find a way early on to reach an agreement with IT that doesn't threaten them or their supremacy as the overall systems architect for the company. This would still allow the development if the hip-pocket resources or a group of people who are IT professionals who are specifically focused on learning application, because there is a difference. The CLO explained that there's a big difference between IT folks that are building billing systems versus IT folks who really understand learning, speak the language, and understand what your overall purpose is in support of the organization. It's a delicate balance because IT folks get nervous when they see little IT guerilla teams springing up around the organization.

Future Study

One recurring theme in this research is the lack of time dedicated by corporations to learners for e-learning during work hours. Most employees find themselves to be totally preoccupied during work hours and are unable to set aside time for e-learning. They have to resort to e-learning at night and on weekends. Corporations need to ask, what is the impact of setting time aside during work hours for e-learning? What is the impact on work-life balance? What is the impact on morale and retention? What is the long-term impact on productivity? A potential rich area for future study is to determine the implication of dedicating time for e-learning during work hours.

Another important theme is that the use of completion rate may not be the appropriate measure for effective learning in the e-learning space. E-learners can go into the courseware and learn just what they need to learn. That could mean just completing a single module or just a slice of the course instead of completing the entire course. Corporations need to ask: How should effective learning be measured when only a portion of the course is completed? How could focus group sessions and controlled experiments be conducted to explore e-learning behaviors? How could courses be divided further into smaller slices? A potential rich area of research is to determine how completion rate should really be defined in e-learning.

6

CONCLUSION

Summary

Given the demand for just-in-time learning, a global workforce and the rapid movement toward a digital society, e-learning is increasingly becoming an essential component of a corporate training program to help corporations achieve their strategic goals and competitive advantage. This research explored the extent to which e-learning is feasible and the decision criteria used to determine the appropriate level of e-learning. It examined how much e-learning is being developed and implemented at IBM and other corporations. It explored the rationale for the various e-learning applications. This research also examined how effectiveness of e-learning is determined. IBM was selected because it has a large number of employees and it operates globally, conditions that lend themselves to e-learning. Because of this, IBM has invested substantial resources in implementing e-learning. Because of IBM's global presence, it presents an excellent forum within which the applicability of e-learning can be tested. This research explored the integration of strategy, development, implementation, and the effectiveness of e-learning.

IBM is an early adopter that used e-learning as a tool for training its workforce. IBM is a renowned global technology company that provides computer hardware, software, and consulting services. IBM and other corporations each has its own rationale for and approach to using e-learning. Each corporation provides a unique context for leveraging e-learning to train its employees. Each has its share of lessons learned. Each contributes to the evolution of corporate e-learning in its own way. IBM represents a rich source for learning about how e-learning can be implemented.

This research includes a review of literature on e-learning, including books and articles written about e-learning at IBM, a review of internal company documents, and forty interviews by the author. The study began by posing a series of key research questions about how corporate e-learning is created.

- Why e-learning?
- How is e-learning developed?
- How is e-learning implemented?
- How is effectiveness determined?
- What lessons are learned?

In order to understand how corporate e-learning is created, these questions were used as a framework to review the literature and to conduct interviews with e-learning professionals and managers at IBM and other corporations. The responses to each of these questions and the combined responses to all these questions provide the overall framework for examples of how e-learning can be created at IBM and other corporations. E-learning experiences should be viewed in the context of their business objectives and operating environments.

Research Findings

Why E-Learning?

It's Cheaper and Faster

E-learning is used because it's cheaper, faster and it is a means to reach a global workforce in a timely manner. There are not enough classrooms to accommodate 300,000 employees. IBM and other corporations use it because it's strategic and because it's economical.

Another corporation I examined wants to use e-learning as a platform for their global business and reach the global workforce in the most efficient manner. They want speed to market.

Another corporation I examined wants to standardize its training so that its splicers have a common set of skills to respond to emergencies all across the country during storms. They want splicing to be taught the same way so that workers can help one another across the country. Whatever the reasons, the bottom line is that e-learning must make sense for a given circumstance. It must be the best solution for that application.

Innovation

IBM is in the business of developing computer technology, so there is a natural focus on developing and creating innovative ways of using technology. IBM's most recent On Demand e-learning strategy is a novel way of applying e-learning. This latest strategy is simple, but its implication can be quite significant. The idea behind On Demand is to bring learning immediately to the learner at the desktop at the workplace. On-demand learning is a revolutionary way of approaching learning. Traditionally, learning is done sequentially: Do the learning first and then apply it in the workplace. On demand views learning from the perspective of the workplace first. It is done on a real- time basis and addresses the challenges that a person faces everyday. It provides a tool to solve that particular problem at that instant.

How Is E-Learning Developed?

E-Learning Partners Must Take Ownership

Both the stated business objectives and the expected learning outcome must be clear from the start. Subject-matter experts, designers, developers, infrastructure specialists, and technologists must work collaboratively during the process of creating e-learning. There must be commitment on the part of the corporation, instructors, and learners. The appropriate process must be in place. A proper learning environment and the right kind of technology are required.

Content Must Be Relevant

The content must be relevant, framed in the right context and have quality. Content should be helpful to learners in their work performance. The design must be interactive, engaging, and intuitive. Content must be properly matched with a delivery system, so learners can have ready access. There can be no technical glitches because learners will not come back if there are glitches that cause frustration. Technical requirements include bandwidth, interoperability, access, browser and software compatibility. Everyone wants high touch, so interactivity and collaboration are important ingredients. E-learning should be kept simple. The platform should be standardized so learners don't have to deal with multiple LMSs or deal with problems of access. It should be easy to navigate.

IBM's Four Tier Approach: What Content Should Be Delivered via E-Learning?

IBM's four-tier model is an excellent way to assess when e-learning should be used and when classroom learning should be used. The first three tiers fall within the domain of e-learning. Tier one refers to learning from information. Tier two calls for learning from interaction. Tier three is learning from collaboration. The first two levels are done through self-paced e-learning. The third is done through synchronous e-learning where people are gathering at the same time and at the same or different locations. Tier four calls for learning from collocation. This tier is reserved for face-to-face sessions (IBM 2004).

Purchase versus Build

IBM and other corporations generally purchase libraries of software from vendors on standardized products. Most corporations are not interested in reinventing the wheel. They concentrate their internal development efforts in areas that are uniquely related to their businesses. IBM developed Basic Blue because it is training that incorporates IBM culture.

Another corporation developed its own executive-development courses. It will buy off the shelf if available, but it will build if the corporation has unique requirements or when outside vendors don't have the skills to develop these programs.

Another corporation I examined developed its own e-learning program for splicing, which is unique to its business.

How Is E-Learning Implemented?

Voluntary and Cuddled

The belief that if you build it, they will come fails time and again unless e-learning has the right content and context to attract learners. IBM and other corporations took a voluntary, instead of mandatory, approach for implementation. E-learning was a major change for learners, and many were not accustomed to the use of technology for learning. Learners were given 24/7 access to a catalogue of courses. They were given proper equipment and provided with the right delivery system. They were guided along the way as they were getting acclimated to e-learning. Online advisors and help desks were available, and they responded to the learners' needs promptly. Their responsiveness and timeliness gave learners a sense of ownership in the process. There were also tutors in learning centers to provide support to learners. The early adopters became the best ambassadors for e-learning. Their word of mouth was more powerful to peers than directives coming from the corporation. Acceptance was found to be a bottom up process.

Winning Over Instructors

Another component of implementation is acceptance by the instructors. Teaching an e-learning class is substantially different from teaching an instructor-led in-class session. The instructors of e-learning are dealing with a faceless audience, so it takes much more effort to ensure interactivity. They have to make sure that learners are in fact getting mastery of the material and that they are not tuning out. The instructor's role is shifting from sage on the stage to facilitator on the sideline. Transitioning from an instructor-led class to e-learning is no easy task. IBM and other corporations provide training to instructors on the new media. Instructors are given training in how to involve the audience and how to handle electronic technology. They have to be persuaded that classroom instruction is not always practical or affordable and that e-learning makes sense in certain applications. Satisfaction in e-learning comes from knowing that many more people are being reached and that knowledge is being passed onto many more people than classrooms can accommodate. Further, instructors should be given the opportunity to be involved in curriculum design so that they can get a sense of ownership. Instructors are an important link in the delivery of e-learning to learners. They have to make sure that the material is delivered to the learners in an effective way. They must know and understand the delivery techniques.

Corporate Support: Sustained Commitment

Corporate support is another important part of the implementation process. E-learning requires substantial investment and commitment on the part of the company. There will be some growing pains, so the financial support has to be sustained over time. Also, it's advisable to undertake fewer but more substantial projects instead of numerous minor projects. Corporate support must also include a culture of encouragement and reward. E-learning needs buy-in from all levels of the corporation. It needs managers to know that e-learning is a feasible way to accomplish business objectives. Culture will take time to evolve. A reward system that is structured around the importance of learning to the corporation will help pave the way for that change. Culture is something that will either stymie or enhance the growth of e-learning.

A supportive environment will provide the proper equipment, facilities, infrastructure, and training. A supportive environment also means appreciation for learning and providing time for learning.

One problem area for IBM is that its employees are so preoccupied with their normal workload that they can't find time to do e-learning during work hours, so they tend to do e-learning during off hours and weekends. Employees are simply resigned to the fact that their jobs are not 9 to 5 jobs and that they have to learn on their own time in order to stay competitive. The CLO understands that this is an issue that runs counter to what the company has been saying about encouraging learning. It runs counter to work- life balance. This is an issue that IBM needs to address and find feasible ways to carve out time and space during work hours. IBM should measure the cost/benefit of allowing employees to take courses during work hours. That is, can workers be more productive with a better work-life balance? Is the stress of off-hour learning deleterious to the personal lives of employees and does it, thus, negatively affect corporate performance? What is the impact of fatigue, burnout, illness, and family discord? Do corporations have a duty to be concerned about the welfare of their employees beyond bottom line considerations?

Other corporations also said that their employees typically have to find time to work on e-learning during nights and weekends.

Learning Management System—Importance of Interoperability

Another important element of implementation of e-learning is the LMS. This is a common platform where learners can get access to courses and their training progress report. It is a portal where information can be shared across the company. IBM had to consolidate multiple systems into a common LMS. Another corporation I examined built its own LMS. The

LMS is a way to keep track of learners' performance and progress on courses. The online advisor is there to answer questions. There are also learning communities that are available to exchange ideas and discuss issues with experts who have interests in the same disciplines. A common platform is key to success.

How Is Effectiveness Determined?

Kirkpatrick Model: What and How to Measure

IBM and other corporations generally follow the four levels of measurement devised by Kirkpatrick. Level 1 is a survey of learner satisfaction. The feedback here is important to enhance the course work and also to improve learning. Level 2 is a survey of mastery of the material. Each course must have a purpose and must have a stated set of skills to be learned. These should be identified before the course is designed. Upon completion of a course, the mastery test will determine if the required skills were learned. Level 3 evaluates whether the learned information is being applied in the workplace. This is more challenging, because it is difficult to isolate the single element of e-learning from employees' other skills. However, self-reporting from learners and instructors is very helpful in the process. There are limitations to self-reporting, but if a series of questions are asked and there are logical links to responses to these questions, useful information about how well learners learned can be inferred. Level 4 is the measurement of cost savings or rate of ROI. There are two components to this equation. The first is the avoided cost and the second is revenue gained from increased productivity. The first is an easier task. It involves calculations of traveling and hotel expenses avoided. The second is more difficult to measure. It calls for an estimation of increase in revenue because of the additional time that learners have saved with which they can generate revenue. For example, a sales representative who learns through e-learning has more time to sell products and services.

The Ultimate Measure—Customer Satisfaction

IBM, with its ACE model, actually went beyond Kirkpatrick's four-level model by introducing customer satisfaction as the fifth element. The theory is that if the employee is satisfied with his training, he will manifest that satisfaction in providing better service to ultimate customers.

Satisfaction of ultimate customers means greater consumption and greater return of customers. By word of mouth, it could also translate into new customers. This model includes learner accountability, instructor responsibility, management support, and enabling processes.

What Lessons Are Learned?

Importance of Feedback and Continuous Improvement

Many corporations, universities, and vendors were caught up in the hype of the Internet bubble five years ago. They were motivated by a combination of optimism, greed, and willful ignorance of history that led them to believe that information technology would create a permanent bull market (Unsworth 2004). When the bubble burst, people started to ask why the high promise of e-learning failed. IBM and other corporations had their own shares of growing pains. The lessons they learned will be instructive to others. Because e-learning involves process, content, technology, assessment, design, integration, and implementation, it can easily be derailed by any of these components. Broadly speaking, failure of e-learning can occur at the learner level, the product level, or the organization level.

Learner Level—Avoid Technical Difficulties

For learners, technical difficulty is a major obstacle. If they don't have the right equipment, software, or bandwidth, they can easily be frustrated. If they have a hard time accessing the course, they will be turned off and not come back. Natural fear of technology can be an obstacle to some learners, so small, incremental steps need to be taken to meet those learners at their skill levels. Learners also must be persuaded that they are not being deprived, and that e-learning is not necessarily a cheaper way of learning but that it is used as one of many methods to optimize training. They must realize that multitasking will be a hindrance to learning. When they are using e-learning, they should give their undivided attention. They should not be checking e-mail and taking phone calls at the same time. Learner motivation and accountability is key to success in e-learning.

For learners, lack of familiarity with e-learning is another major obstacle. IBM and other corporations took a voluntary rather than mandatory approach to e-learning. This eased the transition from classroom learning to e-learning. An important lesson is not to make courses mandatory until there has been at least some level of acceptance and buy-in by learners.

Product Level—Avoid Poor Content/Design

At the product level, learners should not be indiscriminately inundated with hundreds of courses. That will not add value to their learning and will be viewed as a lack of focus on the part of the corporation. The product should have the relevant content and context. It has to help employees better perform their jobs. For those who are accustomed to in-class training, e-learning is a challenge. As such, design is a critical component to make sure that the techniques used are the best to get the material across to learners. It should be engaging and interactive. It should build in a sufficient number of questions, quizzes, and discussion forums to hold the attention of the learners. Unless the product is relevant and engaging, learners will not use it. Because you build it doesn't mean they will come. Continuous feedback from learners and trainers and continuous improvement of courses are needed to make inroads on e-learning.

Corporate Level—Avoid Half-Hearted Commitment

At the corporate level, support must come in the form of substantial investment and the appropriate learning environment. A strong learning culture is needed for success. Corporate culture means embracing the value of e-learning at all levels of the company. A corporate learning organization needs to have an e-learning strategy; it must support learners and instructors, involve IT, and form partnerships with line organizations. Corporate support must include ways to allow learners time for using e-learning. This is an area that corporations have struggled with because employees must learn during off hours. They must do so because they are so preoccupied during work hours or they have field jobs that don't permit them to settle down in a single location. Ted Hoff, CLO of IBM, said, "The practical reality of life a lot of times is basically to do e-learning at 10 P.M. at night after you finish your e-mails. Do we at different sites set aside space that we just use for learning where you can get away from the phone and go conduct it? So some one can say to their boss I am going to go over and do this for three hours? We don't have this one figured out yet" (Hoff, personal interview, 2004).

Creating E-Learning—Integration of Components

Creating e-learning involves building a business case and developing, implementing, and measuring the effectiveness of e-learning. Each of the steps has to be done well, but all the steps must collectively be integrated into the whole. No step can be undertaken without considering the impact on other steps. For example, when e-learning is being designed, the project manager must know what to measure. Otherwise, what the project manager wants to measure after the design is completed might not align with the initial design. And when e-learning is being designed, the project manager must know what delivery system is needed and what IT support will be required.

So just how is e-learning created in corporations? To begin with, the development of e-learning starts with a clear set of stated business objectives. The purpose of the e-learning solution is to enable learners in the organizations to accomplish those business objectives. That e-learning solution includes content, design, delivery, implementation, measurements, and feedback. Content has to be relevant and presented in the right context. Subject-matter experts are the drivers behind content. Content must be suitable for e-learning. If it's highly interactive, face-to-face learning may be more appropriate. Design must involve adult-learning specialists and Web technologists to make sure that the content is presented in a way that is most engaging and conducive to learning. Delivery of the content has to be put in place so that learners can access e-learning courseware. Delivery systems include appropriate learning architecture, technical infrastructure, bandwidth, and computer software and hardware. A common platform is imperative so information can be shared across the organization. Interoperability is key. Technical difficulties can frustrate learners and derail adoption of e-learning. Implementation requires careful nurturing of learners, buy-in from instructors, and strong support from the organization. E-learning courses should be designed to meet learners at their skill levels. Instructors should be trained on delivery techniques in this new environment. Organizations should be committed to provide funding, encouragement, time, and equipment to learn. Measuring the effectiveness of e-learning solutions is critical to provide feedback needed for continuous improvement. A well-defined learning organization structure with strong leadership facilitates successful implementing of e-learning.

However, there is no one size that fits all. The key ingredients for a successful e-learning program can be met in different ways, depending on the nature of the organizations, their business environment, available resources, and the extent of applicability of e-learning. Thus, IBM and other corporations each has its own unique e-learning solutions. Strategic vision, clear business objectives, well-defined learning organization, strong leadership, corporate support, prudent use of e-learning, quality of content, ease of access, interoperability, accountability of learners and instructors and a well-defined measurement system all matter. Ignoring any of these key ingredients can lead to failure. IBM and other corporations have learned ample lessons, and these should serve as an important reference to those who are implementing e-learning.

Research Findings Summary

The overall conclusions that emerged as a result of key research questions are summarized below:

- First, there must be a stated business objective behind implementation of e-learning. E-learning should be used only when it makes strategic and economic sense. There could be a variety of reasons such as accessibility, speed, standardization, attraction, and retention for implementing e-learning. The ultimate goal is to provide the highest business impact.
- Second, e-learning is not done for its own sake or for the sake of technology alone. Instead, it is using technology to enable learning. It is a tool to be used along with other means of learning. E-learning is not suitable for every application. Some applications are still better suited for classroom learning. Some applications are suited for a blend of e-learning and classroom learning. The key is to make sure that e-learning is the best way to learn for a particular application. Optimally, it is a way to save costly face-to-face time.
- Third, because e-learning is a dramatic change from classroom learning, content, design, and delivery system must be done in a ways that keep learners engaged. E-learning is more than just putting content on the Web. It should not be just a lengthy page-turner. It should not be just be PowerPoint slides with lines of text.

Reading is not training. Learners want interactions, tests, and contents to hold their interests.

- Fourth, e-learning is not a field of dreams. Because you build it doesn't mean the learners will come. E-learning must be implemented effectively. That means providing support to learners and instructors. That means making sure learners can learn and instructors know how to teach in this new environment. Corporate support must be present to make sure the work environment encourages e-learning. An LMS is also required to establish a common platform for tracking and sharing information.
- Fifth, e-learning must be measured for its effectiveness. It must be measured to see if the stated business objectives are accomplished. No business can afford to implement e-learning without knowing if there is a business case that can be made. Effectiveness means having a feedback mechanism to improve e-learning programs.
- Sixth, there will be many failures in e-learning, but the key is to learn from these failures and not repeat the same mistakes. Failures can occur at the learner level, the product level, or the organizational level. Failure at any of these levels can derail the success of e-learning.

Who Can Benefit from This Research?

Corporations, higher education, and other e-learning providers can all benefit from this research about how e-learning is created. Corporate e-learning and higher education e-learning are basically running on parallel tracks with little intersection. However, the potential of one sector to learn from another is enormous. According to Kjell-Erik Rudestam, a researcher and author on e-learning, corporate trainers and academics can learn much from each other. "The corporate world," he says, "is often more comfortable incorporating new technology into its courses, while veterans of academe who move on to corporate programs bring a valuable commitment to humanizing the workplace" (Read 2002b).

More and more, corporations are using e-learning as a tool for learning. Higher education is no different. The 2000 survey by the Campus Computing Project indicated that more than 40 percent of all college courses now use Web resources, up from 11 percent in 1995. Furthermore, the Massachusetts Institute of Technology announced that it will spend

$100 million to place courses on the Web so its courseware can be accessed by the public at no charge (Kelly 2001). Corporations are making substantial investments in research and development and in assessing the effectiveness of e-learning. Universities can learn from their practice and experience. Corporations have the technology and the universities have the know-how in teaching. They can potentially reap substantial benefits by working together and pooling their resources.

IBM is a pioneer and leader in implementing e-learning. E-learning has already made a difference in how their employees learn and work, as evidenced by their significant level of adoption. E-learning already represents 48 percent of learning at IBM. The experiences at IBM and other corporations viewed in the context of the nature of their business, their objectives, their operating environments, and their corporate cultures, offer a rich guide on corporate e-learning. As bandwidth increases and technology advances, the role of e-learning will continue to increase in corporate learning. IBM has already gained a considerable amount of practical experience from their e-learning programs in the past five years. They will undoubtedly continue to be innovative and make advances in e-learning in the future.

APPENDIX A: INTERVIEW PROTOCOL

Why E-Learning?
- What is the strategic reason for doing it?
- What is the role of technology in e-learning?
- How do size, geography, and speed come in to play?
- What is the role of accessibility?
- What is the expectation on investment and productivity?

How Is E-Learning Developed?
- How do you select content and design for e-learning?
- How do you build work practice into e-learning?
- How do you consider the target audience?
- How do you build collaboration and interactivity into e-learning?
- How do you balance classroom training and e-learning?
- How do you determine how to deliver the content to target audiences?
- How do you decide what technology to use?
- Who are all the professionals involved in the development?
- Who develops e-learning?
- Do you do it internally, in partnership with others or do you outsource?

How Is E-Learning Implemented?
- How do you make sure that e-learning will be accepted?
- What type of corporate support is required?
- How do you describe your learning culture?

- How do you bring about culture change?
- How do you prepare instructors?
- How do you support the learners?
- How do you market e-learning?
- How do you launch e-learning?
- How do you keep track of the learners' progress?

How Is Effectiveness Determined?
- What are your criteria for evaluating e-learning?
- What types of measurements do you use?
- What are the difficulties in measuring effectiveness?
- What is the feedback from learners, instructors, and managers?
- How does e-learning change the way you do business?

What Lessons Are Learned?
- What problems are encountered on the learner side?
- What problems are encountered with e-learning products?
- What cultural hurdles need to be overcome?
- What problems with corporate support are involved?
- What are the difficult areas to apply e-learning and why?
- What technology hurdles are encountered?

APPENDIX B: PERSONAL INTERVIEWS

IBM

1. Linda Anderson, Facilitator for Basic Blue IBM, Management Development
2. Crystal Arrington, Learning Leader, IBM Corporate
3. Mike Giersch, Vice President, Strategic Planning, IBM Corporate
4. Teresa Golden, Vice President, Marketing and Strategy
5. Ted Hoff, Vice President, Chief Learning Officer
6. Nancy Kaufman, Learning Leader, IBM Corporate
7. Chak Lau, Program Director, Learning Effectiveness Measurement
8. Nancy J. Lewis, Vice President, On Demand Learning
9. Bob MacGregor, Manager of Basic Blue, IBM Management Development
10. Matt McLaughlin, Learning Leader, Sales and Distribution
11. Denise Murphy, Administrator, Project Lead for Basic Blue for Manger Training Program
12. Beverly Sanford, Learning Leader, IBM Corporate
13. Jim Soltis, Facilitator of Basic Blue, IBM Management Development
14. Maria Amelia O. Troise, Workplace Specialty Leader, Software Group, Lotus, Student in Basic Blue
15. John Wattendorf, Program Director, Management Development Learning Design
16. Robert Weintraub, Manager for Global Services, Learning Strategy
17. Fran Zinzi, Program Manager, IBM Learning Organization

REFERENCES

Adkins, S. S. (June 2003). "The Brave New World of Learning." *Training & Development* 57(6).

Aldrich, C. (August 2000). "Customer-Focused E-Learning: The Drivers." *Training Development* 54(8), 34–37.

Bagshaw, M., and Bagshaw, C. (2002). "Radical Self-Development: A Bottom Up Perspective." *Industrial and Commercial Training (Guilsborough)* 34(4/5), 194–197.

Barron, T. (December 2000). "Getting IT support for E-Learning." *Training & Development* 54(12), 32–37.

Beamish, N., Armistead, C., Watkinson, M., & and Armfield, G. (2002). "The Deployment of E-Learning in UK/European Corporate Organizations." *European Business Journal* 14(3), 105–115.

Berry, J. (November 6, 2000). "Corporate training—The E-Learning Center— Companies Are Using Metrics to Justify E-Learning's Impact on Strategic Business Goals." *Internet Week* 836, 61.

Bersin, J. (March 2002). "Measuring, E-Learning's Effectiveness: A Five Step Program for Success." *E-Learning* 3(3), 36–38.

Billington, M. (January 2003). "Training/Learning: What Fits Your Company." *Chief Learning Officer Magazine.*

Bolch, M. (September 2002). "E-Learning Comes of Age." *Training* 39(9), 114–119.

Brannick, M. (January 2003). "Measures of Learning Effectiveness." *Chief Learning Officer.*

Broadbent, B. (December 2000). "Anyone, Anywhere, Anytime." *OH & S Canada* 16(8), 50–51.

Burns, T. (February 2005). "E-Learning: The Future of Quality Training." *Quality Progress*, 38(2), 50–56.

Carnevale, D (March 2002). "Colleges Tailor Online Degree for Individual Companies." *The Chronicle of Higher Education.*

Caudron, S. (January 2001). "Training's Hot." *Training & Development,* 55(1), 30–35.

CIO Magazine, http://www.cio.com/summaries/enterprise/knowledge/index. html.

Cirillo, R., and Silverstein, D. (2002, 4/3/1). "Plug into E-Learning." *VARBusiness,* 18(5).

Clarke, T., and Hermens, A. (2001). "Corporate Developments and Strategic Alliances in E-Learning." *Education & Training* 43(4/5), 256–268.

Coleman, A. December (2001). "Clicking into Place." *Director* 55(5), 70–72.

Cone, J. W., and Robinson, D. G. (August 2001). The power of E-performance. *Training & Development* 55(8), 32–41.

Creswell, J. W. (2003). *Research design qualitative, quantitative and mixed methods approaches. Thousand Oaks,* Calif.: Sage Publications.

Cummings, B. (April 2001). "Channeling Online E-Learning." *Sales and Marketing Management* 153(4), 68.

Del Vecchio, G., and Bonthrone, D. (October 2003). "Sales Force Effectiveness through E-Learning." *Pharmaceutical Executive (Eugene),* 23(10), 106.

Devi, C. (October 1, 2001). "Setting Up Right E-Learning Environment." *New Straits Times.*

Dobbs, K. (October 2000a). "The Coming Shake Sut in E-Learning." *Training* 37(10), 114–118.

Dobbs, K. (September 2000b). "What the Online World Needs Now: Quality." *Training,* 37(9), 84–94.

Donovan, T. (April 2003). "IBM to Save $1bn with 1m-User LMS." *ITT Training.*

Driscoll, M. (July 2003). "How E-Learning Can Facilitate Rapid Compliance." *Bank Systems & Technology* 40(6), 44.

Egan, D. (May 2002). "Need Funding for an E-Learning Initiative? Think Like a CEO." *Training & Development* 56(5), 94–98.

Elswick, J. (June 15, 2002). "Staying the Training Course." *Employee Benefit News,* 16(8), 23–24.

Erikson, F. (1986). *Qualitative Methods in Research and Teaching: Handbook of Research on Teaching.* 3rd ed. New York: Macmillan.

Ettinger, A. (2005). "Xerox Takes a Strategic Approach to E-Learning." *Human Resources Management Digest* 13(1), 6–8.

Evans, K. B. (2002). "E-Learning in Action at Xerox Europe." *Training & Management Development Methods,* 16(3), 501–506.

Franklin, S. (October 2003). "A Vendor-Provided Case Study." *Training & Development* 57(10), 66–67.

Freivalds, J. (November 2000). "Coursework Network." *Export Today's Global Business* 16(11).

Galagan, P. A. (December 2000). "The E-Learning Revolution." *Training & Development* 54(12), 24–30.

Galagan, P. A. (February 2001). "Mission E-Possible." *Training & Development*, 55(2), 46–56.

Gale, S. F. (August 2002). "Measuring the ROI of E-Learning." *Workforce (Costa Mesa)*, 81(8), 74–76.

Gallaher, J., and Wentling, T. L. (2004). "The Adoption of E-Learning Across Professional Groups." *Performance Improvement Quarterly* 17(3), 66–85.

Galloway, D. L. (April 2005). "Evaluating Distance Delivery and E-Learning." *Performance Improvement* 44(4), 21–27.

Gareiss, D. (February 26, 2001). "E-Learning around the World." *Information Week (Manhasset)* 826, 63–64.

General Electric Company. (2002). General Electric Annual Report (Chairman's letter to shareholders).

George, T., and McGee, M.K. (2003). "E-Learning Helps Companies Capture the Knowledge of Retiring Employees and Gain Competitive Edge." *Information Week*.

Gillette, B. (March 2003). "Providers Eager to Embrace E-Learning to Ensure Regulatory Training." *Managed Health Care Executive* 13(3), 40–41.

Glesne, C., and Peshkin, A. (1992). *Becoming Qualitative Researchers: An Introduction*. White Plains, N.Y.: Longman.

Gold, M. (April 2003). "Enterprise E-Learning." *Training & Development* 57(4), 28–33.

Goldwasser, D. (January 2001). Beyond ROI. *Training*, 38(1), 82–86.

Goodridge, E. (January 28, 2002). "IBM and Microsoft Send Employees Back to School." *InformationWeek* 873, 30.

Grimes, A. (March 12, 2001). "The Hope and the Reality: Big Money Is Pouring into the Business of Education; but It's too Soon to Tell whether There Will Be Any Payoff." *The Wall Street Journal (New York), Eastern ed.*, E-Commerce (A Special Report) R.6.

Groves, S. (March/April 2002). "Training on a Tight Rope." *Information Management Journal* 36(2), 7.

Harris, J. (October 9–12, 2001). "Case Study: Fast, Cost-Effective Method to Deliver Training." ASTD Techknowledge Conference & Exposition.

Harris, P. (February 2003). "ROI of E-Learning." *Training & Develpment*, 57(2), 30–35.

Hartley, D. (September 2000). "Looking for a Supplier." *Training & Development* 54(9), 26–30.

Hartley, D. E. (April 2001). "E-valuation: Pricing E-Learning." *Training & Development* 55(4), 24–27.

Hassett, J. (September 2002). "The E-Learning Survival Guide." *Training* 39(9), 120–125.

Henderson, A. J. (2003). *The E-Learning Question and Answer Book*. New York: American Management Association.

Henry, P. (2001). "E-learning Technology, Content and Services." *Education & Training* 43(4/5), 249–256.

Henry, P. (2002). "Learning Enters the Boardroom: Making the Connection between Strategy and Enterprise-Wide Learning." *Industrial and Commercial Training* 34(2), 66–69.

Hequet, M., and Johnson, G. (September 2003). "The State of E-Learning Model." *Training* 40(8), 24.

Hicks, S. (December 2000). "Evaluating E-Learning." *Training & Development* 54(12), 75–76.

Hobson, K. (October 15, 2001). "Translation Troubles." *U.S. News & World Report* 131(15), 58.

Hoff, T. (2002). *IBM learning initiative programs that incorporates the "blended E-learning model, IBM's 4 tier model."* IBM learning initiative, CLO Armonk, N.Y.

Hoff, T. (January 2003). (Thoff@us.ibm.com). (IBM CLO profile).

Hollis, E. (2002). "PTC: Blended Learning for Sales Training." *Chief Learning Officer Magazine.*

Hollis, E. (February 26, 2003). "Selling E-Learning to Non-Technical Learners." *Chief Learning Officer Magazine.*

Holman, G., and Macpherson, A. (2005). "E-learning in the Corporate University." *Journal of European Industrial Training* 25(1), 75–90.

Honey, P. (2001). "E-Learning: A Performance Appraisal and Some Suggestions for Improvement." *The Learning Organization* 8(5), 200–202.

IBM. *About IBM,* http://www.ibm.com/ibm/us/.

IBM. (2002). *IBM Annual Report 2002* (Chairman's letter to shareholders).

IBM (2004). IBM Learning Solutions 2004.

Imel, S. (2002). "E-Learning. Trends and Issues Alert." Office of Educational Research and Improvement (ED), Washington, DC.

Ingram, H., Sandelands, E., and Teare, R. (2001). "Building High Performance Learning: A Focus on Career Results and the Business Bottom Line." *The Learning Organization* 8(5), 211–220.

Johne, M. (February 2003). "Virtual Environments." *CMA Management* 76(10), 28–32.

Kelly, T. M. (July 13, 2001). "Before Plugging in, Consider Your Options." *The Chronicle of Higher Education.*

Khirallah, D. R., and Kolbasuk, M. M. (2000, 22/5/2). "A New Way to Learn?" *Information Week,* 787.

King, W. R. (Fall 2001). "Developing an IS Education Strategy." *Information Systems Management* 18(4), 77.

Krell, E. (December 2002). "Calculating Success." *Training* 39(12), 46–50.

Kruse, K. (November 2003). "Tech Trends Impacting E-Learning." *Chief Learning Officer* 2(7), 19.

Laine, L. (June 2003). "Is E-Learning Effective for IT Training." *Training & Development* 57(6), 56–61.

Leacock, T. (2005). "Building a Sustainable E-Learning Development Culture." *The Learning Organization* 12(4), 355–367.

Lewis, N. J., and Orton, P. (June 2000). "The Five Attributes of Innovative E-Learning." *Training & Development* 54(3), 47–51.

Light, R. J., Singer, J. D., and Willett, J. B. (1990). *By Design: Planning Research on Higher Education*. Cambridge, Massachusetts: Harvard University Press.

Little, B. (September 2003a). "Building a Brand in a Small Scale." *E-Learning Age*, 44–45.

Little, B. (2003b). "Six Sigma Techniques Improve the Quality of E-Learning." *Industrial and Commercial Training (Guilborough)* 35(2/3), 104.

Lovelace, P. (July 2003). "Lessons Gleaned from E-Learning Peers." *Credit Union Magazine* 69(7), 16.

Lynch, S. (2002). "Environment—The CLO's Role: Balancing the Learning Mix in Outsourced Environments." *Chief Learning Officer Magazine.*

Lytras, M. D., Pouloudi, A., and Poulymenakou, A. (2002). "Knowledge Management Convergence—Expanding Learner Frontiers." *Journal of Knowledge Management* 6(1), 40–51.

Macpherson, A., Homan, G., and Wilkinson, K. (2005). "The Implementation and Use of E-Learning in the Corporate University." *The Journal of Workplace Learning* 17(1/2), 33–48.

Maisto, M., and Rajendran, R. K. (August/September 2002). "Content at the Speed of Light." *E-Learning* 3(8), 16–21.

Mantyla, K. (2001). *Blending E-Learning: The Power Is in the Mix*. Alexandria, Va: ASTD.

Marsan, C. (2003, 13/10). "GE Motors along with E-Learning Software." *Network World* 20(41), 27.

Marshall, C., and Rossman, G. (1999). *Designing Qualitative Research*, 3rd ed. Thousand Oaks, California: Sage.

Mauger, S. (May 2002). "E-Learning 'is about people not technology'." *Adult Learning (England)* 13(7), 9–11.

Maxey, L. (May 2002). "The Changing Landscape of Learning." *ASTD.*

Maxwell, J. (1996). *Qualitative Research Design: An Interactive Approach*, 3rd ed. Thousand Oaks, California: Sage.

McConnell, D. (May 2002). "The Experience of Collaborative Assessment in E-Learning." *Studies in Continuing Education* 24(1), 73–92.

Meister, J. C. (February 9, 2001). "The Brave New World of Corporate Education." *The Chronicle of Higher Education.*

Moore, K. (2001, 3/9/3). "E-learning Gets Boost from IBM." *InfoWorld* 23(35/36).

Moore, K. (2003, 17/2/1). "Web Services Tap E-Learning." *InfoWorld* 25(7).

Munzer Eli. (October 2002). "Q & A with Eli Munzer." *Thomson NETg*, 1–3.

Oakes, K. (September 2002). "Is This Industry for Real?" *Training* 39(9), 154.

Oakes, K. (January 2003a). "E-Learning." *Training & Development*, 57(1), 64–66.

Oakes, K. (April 2003b). "E-Learning." *Training & Development* 57(4), 72–77.

Oakes, K. (July 2003c). "E-Learning." *Training & Development* 57(7), 17–20.

Oakes, K., and Rengarajan, R. (June 2002a). "The Hitchhiker's Guide to Knowledge Management E-Learning." *Training & Development* 56(6), 75–77.

Oakes, K., and Rengarajan, R. (September 2002b). "Synching Up with Virtual Classrooms: E-Learning." *Training and Development*, 56(9), 57–60.

Oakes, K., and Rengarajan, R. (November 2002c). "E-Learning." *Training & Development* 56(11), 58–61.

Page, I. (2005). "How to Purchase Successful E-Learning; Top Tips for Training Buyers." *Training & Management Development Methods* 19(1–5), 627–632.

Pantazis, C. (September 2002). "Maximizing E-Learning to Train the 21st Century Workforce." *Public Personnel Management* 31(1), 21–26.

Paynich, V. (January 2003). "Are No Two Learners Alike?" *E-Learning* 4(1), 6.

Phillips, J. J., and Pope, C. (2001). *In Action Implementing E-Learning Solutions*. *Alexandria*, Va: ASTD.

Piers, L. (2003). "Understanding the Culture of E-Learning." *Industrial and Commercial Training* 35(4/5), 217.

Piskurich, G. M. (2003). *The AMA handbook of E-Learning*. New York: AMACOM.

Pollitt, D. (2005a). "E-Learning Connects Cable & Wireless with Big Cost Savings." *Human Resources Management International Digest* 13(1), 19–20.

Pollitt, D. (2005b). "E-Learning Delivers Management Development Methods." *Training & Management Development Methods* 19(1–5), 639–642.

Pollitt, D. (2005c). "Scottish Power Goes DIY with E-Learning." *Training & Management Development Methods* 19(1–5), 633–637.

Powell, W. (February 2002). "Like Life." *Training & Development* 56(2), 32–38.

Read, B. (April 12, 2002a). "The New Handbook Collects Essays on the Nuts and Bolts of Online Learning." *The Chronicle of Higher Education*.

Read, B. (September 20, 2002b). "A Scholarly Work from Blackboard's Chairman." *The Chronicle of Higher Education*.

Read, B. (September 27, 2002c). "Handbook Examines Online Learning from a Psychological Perspective." *The Chronicle of Higher Education*.

Ready, D. A. (2002). "Learning Styles: What's Right for Your Enterprise?" *Chief Learning Officer Magazine*.

Rianhard, C. (September 2002). "E-Learning." *Business Mexico* 12(9), 57.

Rich, D. (April 2001). "A New Way to Develop Employees." *Electronic Business (Highlands Ranch)* 27(8), 8–9.

Rosenberg, M. J. (2001). *E-Learning Strategies for Delivering Knowledge in the Digital Age*. New York: McGraw-Hill.

Rubenstein, H. (May/June 2003). "Recognizing E-Learning's Potential and Pitfalls." *Learning & Training Innovations* 4(4), 39.

Rubin, H., and Rubin, I. (1995). *Qualitative Interviewing: The Art of Hearing Data.* Thousand Oaks, California.: Sage.

Salopek, J. J. (November 2003). "Changing at the Speed of Light." *Training & Development* 57(11), 28.

Sauer, P. (September 3, 2001). "E-learning Emerges as the Next Horizon in Corporate Training with Promises of Cost-Savings." *Chemical Market Reporter* 260(9), F8–10.

Schank, R. C. (2002). *Designing World-Class E-Learning.* New York: McGraw-Hill.

Schein, E. H. (1999). *The Corporate Culture Survival Guide.* San Francisco, California: John Wiley & Sons, Inc.

Schettler, J. (March 2002). "IBM." *Training* 39(3).

Servage, L. (2005). "Strategizing for Workplace E-Learning: Some Critical Considerations." *The Journal of Workplace Learning* 17(5/6), 304–317.

Sjogren, J., and Fay, J. (June 2002). "Cost Issues in Online Learning: Using 'Competition' to Advantage." *Change* 34(3), 52–57.

Sloman, M. (2002). *The E-Learning Revolution.* New York: AMACOM.

Smedberg, C. (2004). "The Future of E-learning." *Futuristics* 28(1/2), 77–79.

Sosbe, T. (November 2002a). "Fred Harburg—Connecting Motorola with Learning." *Chief Learning Officer Magazine.*

Sosbe, T. (November 2002b). "Xerox and Qwest: Reaching Out to Workers." *Chief Learning Officer Magazine.*

Sparta, P. (July 2002). Before You Buy an E-Learning System, Think Enterprise Wide. *Training & Development* 56(7), 34–35.

Stim, S. (2002). "Eastman Kodak: Success with Grassroots Change Agents." *Chief Learning Officer Magazine.*

Straus, A., and Corbin, J. (1990). *Basics of Qualitative Research: Grounded Theory Procedures and Techniques.* Newbury Park, Calif.: Sage.

Sung, T. (February 2003). "The Bottom Line on Training." *Training &Development* 57(2), 12.

Taylor, C. R. (October 2002). "The Second Wave." *Training & Development* 56(10), 24–28, 30–31.

Thibodeau, P. (July 29, 2002). "Feds Adopt E-Learning to Recruit, Retain Employees." *Computerworld* 36(31), 10.

Thomas, T. (March 19, 2001). "E-Learning Surges as Training Tool." *National Underwriter* 105(12), 11.

Tischell, G. (November 11, 2002). "All Aboard E-Learning at Air, Rail Companies." *InformationWeek* 914, 26.

Torode, C. (November 15, 1999). "Trainers Shift to Choice." *Computer Reseller News* 869, 87–88.

Unsworth, J. M. (2004, 30/1/1). "The Next Wave: Liberation Technology." *The Chronicle of Higher Education* 50(21), B16.

Vam Dam, N. (2004). *The E-Learning Field Book.* New York: McGraw-Hill.

Van der Pool, L. (May 7, 2001). "Hart-boillet." *Adweek* 38(19), 6.

Verespej, M. J. (January 15, 2001). "Click and Learn." *Industry Week* 250(1), 31–34.

Verizon. (2002). *Verizon 2002 Annual Report* (Chairman's letter to shareholders).

Verizon. (January 2003). "Profile of Eli Munzer, Chief E-Learning Architect Verizon Services Corporation." *Thomson NETg News.*

Vest, C. M. (January 30, 2004). "Why MIT Decided to Give Away All Its Course Materials via the Internet." *The Chronicle of Higher Education* 50(21), 20–22.

Voci, E., and Young, K. (2001). "Blended Learning Working in a Leadership Development Programme." *Industrial and Commercial Training,* 33(4/5), 157–161.

Waight, C. L., and Stewart, B. L. (2005). "Valuing the Adult Learner in E-Learning: Part One—A Conceptual Model for Corporate Settings." *The Journal of Workplace Learning* 17(5/6), 337–345.

Wales, E. (April 2003). "Mixed Results for E-Campuses." *IT Training,* 16.

Waller, V. (2001). "Planning E-Learning—The Iceberg Syndrome." *Training & Management Development Method,* 15(5), 537–541.

Wang, F. K. (2002). "Designing a Case-Based E-Learning System: What, How and Why." *Journal on Workplace Learning* 14(1/2), 29–43.

Weaver, P. (August 2002). "Preventing E-Learning Failure." *Training & Development* 56(8), 45–50.

Webb, W. (January 2003a). "Enterprisewide Speed Limits." *Training* 40, 50–53.

Webb, W. (January 2003b). "Who moved my training?" *Training* 40(1), 22–26.

Webdale, J. (September 2003). "Small Firms Can Learn More Online." *Director (London)* 57, 44.

Yeoh, P. (February 19, 2001). "Towards Corporate E-Learning Culture." *New Straits Times.*

Zenger, J., and Uehlein, C. (August 2001). "Why Blended Will Win." *Trainning & Development* 55(8), 54–62.

INDEX